Biblical Wisdom

For a Digital Age

By David Ellingson

Praise and Thanksgiving

Therefore, since we are surrounded by such a great cloud of witnesses, let us throw off everything that hinders and the sin that so easily entangles. And let us run with perseverance the race marked out for us, fixing our eyes on Jesus, the pioneer and perfecter of faith.
St. Paul's Letter to the Hebrews 12:1

If I have seen further it is by standing on the shoulders of giants.
Isaac Newton

This little book would neither have been conceived nor written were it not for a "cloud of witnesses" and "giants." For years the biblical "sound bytes" in this book echoed in my mind. Like the footsteps of giants they rumbled and thundered in my gut. Like bolts of lightning they flashed in my life illuminating the darkness.

There are far too many in the cloud to thank but I would like to praise several witnesses who have cheered me on in my race, giants on whose shoulders I humbly stand.

- The preaching and poetry of my faith-filled parents, Richard and Leila Ellingson
- The teaching and mentoring of Weston Noble, Henri Nouwen, George Johnson and Merton Strommen
- The partnership and friendship of Susan Houglum and Mark Jackson

Special thanks in the preparation of this book goes to Pam Gompf for assisting in development of the learning activities and Anne Reinisch in cover and interior design.

Soli Deo Gloria

The Problem
and the Opportunity

Like Sheep without a Shepherd

One of my favorite places to hang out is Third Place Books. As its name suggests Third Place Books is a bookstore but it is more. There's a food court with a wonderful variety of cuisine from around the world. There is also a stage which is used on weekend nights for musicians, poets, dancers, and authors to share their gifts with an appreciative audience. At any time of day or night people gather to read, play cards, eat, converse, and be together. That's the idea of Third Place. Other "third places" might be a café, a pub, a town square, or a church. Sociologist Ray Oldenberg suggests we humans need three primary places in our life: our home, our workplace/school, and a "third place" where people from all walks of life interact, experience, and celebrate our common humanity and our diversity.

In all four gospels a story is told about a gathering of people, a third place. Whether the number was 4,000 or 5,000 the account is of a diverse crowd of folks who were drawn to Jesus and were hungry. But they were not only hungry for food they were hungry for something more and were drawn by Jesus' teaching and his miracles to taste and see. When Jesus saw the crowds he had compassion on them "because they were like sheep without a shepherd." Their immediate need was for food and Jesus provided that in abundance. But they also needed someone to give direction to their lives. The Psalmist describes this kind of shepherding as leading them to green pastures, beside still waters, restoring their souls. It's my sense that more than ever the crowds that gather in today's third places are looking for community, for direction, for hope, for more.

As I enter Third Place books, I see the latest "self-help" books that promise to answer the questions of life. For some it's about self-image, for others healthy nutrition, for still more it's "organic gardening." I love to browse and read in all these areas as they expand my horizons and help me savor another element of life. But as I look around at my fellow learners I sense a desire to go deeper, to address more fundamental issues about meaning and purpose in life. Where are we to turn to receive that "bread of life" and that "living water" which nourishes and satisfies? As people of faith we turn to the Bible, God's Word.

But immediately we encounter a problem. While the Bible is the all-time "best-seller" with over 5 billion copies printed since 1815, it often remains on the shelf collecting dust. Biblical illiteracy is commonplace. Perhaps a generation ago many people knew the basic stories of the Bible and its core message was generally understood. But today most people know little American history, let alone biblical history. In a largely urban society the common rural images in the scriptures fall on deaf ears. We are truly sheep without a shepherd.

And then there are the other "shepherds." Turn on your television or computer, pick up a magazine—many voices are shouting out to buy, to use, to listen, to acquire. More than one trillion dollars are spent each year on advertising in America and much of it is directed at young people. ABC's Nightline program "The Merchants of Cool" describes how corporations send "culture spies" into schools to learn what the "new cool" is so that they can then create the next generation of shoes, shirts, hats, etc., that will make last year's model "uncool" and fuel our need to purchase more and more and more. There are many competing voices in our consumer society and they have enormous power to persuade us to accumulate, to buy, to consume, and to throw away. We are like sheep who do not hear the voice of our Shepherd.

Another challenge to going deeper and addressing fundamental human need is the decreasing attention span of most people. The average adult attention span is 15-20 minutes of focus on a particular subject. With today's young people the span is even shorter. As a teacher I have seen this phenomena in my classroom as students are unable to focus on a topic for any extended period of time. I am forced to break up class time into smaller units and use a greater variety of teaching methods to keep students attention. Many researchers point to increased electronic technology use (cell phones, T.V., computers) as a major factor in decreased attention span. The clinical diagnosis of Attention Deficit Disorder (ADD) is the most serious manifestation of this issue and affects 3-5% of children and adults in America.

Biblical Sound Bytes

Thy Word is a lamp unto my feet and a light unto my path.
PSALM 119:105

I suspect that many who are reading this book have heard this passage from Psalm 119. You may know the musical version made popular by singer Amy Grant a number of years ago. We know deep in our bones that its message is true, that God's word found in the Bible can be a lamp and a light which gives direction to our lives. But amid all the voices which promise light in our busy lives, the Bible sits on the shelf unopened, and the light flickers and fades as we walk our daily path.

Perhaps another reason we don't open our Bibles and let the light shine is we feel inadequate to the task. Our lack of knowledge of the Bible discourages us. We have friends who really know the Bible and by comparison we feel like we are back in Sunday School. Our biblical illiteracy leads us to feel incompetent and we either rely on others to tell us what the Bible says or we abandon the whole enterprise as beyond our ability. Or maybe we have never opened the Bible and the thought overwhelms us because it like learning a whole new language and culture.

Take heart, friend, for you may know more than you realize. You may not know who King Hezekiah was or what the Seventh Commandment is, but much biblical wisdom has found its way into our everyday language and culture. How many of the following expressions are familiar to you?

- It is more blessed to give than to receive. (Acts 20:35)
- The love of money is the root of all evil. (1 Timothy 6:10)
- Be still and know that I am God. (Psalm 46:10)
- To everything there is a season. (Ecclesiastes 3:1)
- Father forgive them for they know not what they do. (Luke 23:34)
- Remember the Sabbath day and keep it holy. (Exodus 21:8)
- What God has joined together, let no one tear asunder. (Mark 10:9)
- And of course, Thy word is a lamp unto my feet and a light unto my path. (Psalm 119:105)

We may not be able to quote chapter and verse but we certainly have heard and know these expressions. Perhaps it was your grandmother who shared the verse. Or maybe it was your pastor. Could it have been quoted by a politician? How about a professor? Whatever the source, these quotes have found their way through centuries of repetition into the proverbial wisdom we all hold in common. Like a bright ray of light on a dark night, each of these biblical passages gives us direction for our journey.

This kind of short, simple, to-the-point teaching actually is gathered together in an Old Testament book called Proverbs, also a type of biblical teaching and wisdom. Sprinkled throughout the Bible are "proverbial" teachings which address many of the issues we have already discussed. First, we already "know" or are familiar with many of them. Second, they cover a wide range of life-issues. Third, they are applicable to all ages. Fourth, they are relatively easy to remember. And finally, in a digital age of "sound bytes" and short attention spans, they have the potential to be a particularly effective tool for teaching and sharing God's word and providing a light for our daily lives.

Train up a child in the way he/she should go . . .
PROVERBS 22:6

How do we learn and how is faith formed?

I will put my law in their minds and write in on their hearts.
JEREMIAH 31:33

When I was a boy I watched a TV show called "Dragnet" and can still remember the phrase used by detective Jack Friday, when he interrogated a suspect: "Only the facts, ma'm, only the facts." Much of the educational system and approach in our schools is this kind of learning. It is about the facts and focuses on acquiring good, solid, verifiable information. The scientific method is based on discovering truth through verifying a hypothesis (theory) with facts. Memorizing is often used to teach this information, whether scientific data or religious doctrines. This is called cognitive learning and is fundamental to a good education.

When I was in college, my Latin Professor, Dr. Qualley, used this method to teach vocabulary, conjugations, and declensions. We memorized them and recited them in class. One day in class, he said, "Magister Ellingson, you not only need to learn 'by rote' but also 'by heart'." From that day forward we not only recited our memory work, but we had to answer: "What does this mean?"

Martin Luther used this learning method in his Small Catechism when he asked the meaning question. He wanted to get to the heart of the matter. Learning is more than head-knowledge. It is also about our passions and feelings and matters of the heart. This kind of learning is called affective learning. My mother was an English teacher and had learned the poetry of Robert Frost and the soliloquies of William Shakespeare by heart and often used this knowledge to teach my sister and me. When I had a tough decision to make, I remember hearing her recite

Two roads diverged in a wood,
and I-
I took the one less traveled by,
And that has made all the difference.
                    Robert Frost

So learning is not an either-or, it's a both-and of head and heart. Or is there even more?

Faith without works is dead.
JAMES 2:14-16

James, the brother of Jesus, in his letter to Jewish Christians, takes us even deeper into the question of how we learn and how faith is formed. His conviction was that head and heart are important, but ultimately action is the test of the learning of faith. It's more than saying the right words and believing the correct doctrine. The ultimate test of faith is living it and practicing it. This kind of education is often called experiential education and is based on significant research that documents that we learn best by doing. My numbers aren't exact, but I tell my students to remember 20-40-60-80. What does this mean? We remember approximately 20% of what we hear, 40% of what we see, 60% of what we do and 80% of what we hear, see, do, and tell about! This explains the transformative power of service-learning as people learn and grow through service with and for others. This is the most effective and life-changing education because it is holistic. It involves the whole person: head, heart, and hands.

Today's Examples:

"You deserve a break today." It's certainly not from the Bible, but wisdom aimed at a busy American consumer (women?) suggesting that they deserve a break from cooking today. Where? McDonalds?

As mentioned earlier, there are many voices competing for our attention and at the top of the list are advertisers selling a variety of goods and services to a consumer society. The power of the jingle or musical phrase has long been understood by the business community. If we hear the jingle frequently it begins playing automatically in our heads. I bet you know the current McDonald's slogan: "I'm loving it!" You barely had to think about it. It is estimated an American child views an average of 10,000 food advertisements each year. The strategy has worked well and is partly responsible for the growing epidemic of obesity in our fast-food nation. Mass media understands shortened attention spans and competing voices and gets its message across in sound bytes. Such pithy sentences, packed with essential information, Mark Twain described as a "minimum of sound to a maximum of sense." Politicians make good use of such phrases to crystallize their core beliefs and ideas. After World War II, General Dwight Eisenhower was elected president under "Peace with Prosperity" and, more recently, Barack Obama was elected with "Yes, we can!"

Most recently the Digital Age has furthered the process of communication through email, texting, twitter, and Facebook. Email made it possible to receive and send multiple short messages instantaneously. Only a few short years ago a professional may have written several letters during a work day. Now, through email, it is possible to send scores of messages in a day. Texting has further shorted messaging and by 2010 the average American teenager was sending and receiving over 3,000 text message each month (or over 100 per day). Twitter, a form of mini-blogging launched in 2006, now has over 300 million members with over 300 mini-messages (called tweets) transmitted each day. And Facebook, a social networking resource started in 2004 which shares short messages on both private and public walls, now has over 800,000,000 users worldwide and represents 41% of the U.S. population. Such messaging ranges from personal (updates) to political (Arab Spring).

In a largely "biblically illiterate" society with multiple voices competing for a "shortened attention spans", it would be easy to simply give up or give in to all that is going on around us. But in every generation people of faith have found powerful, appropriate, and creative ways to share, learn, and apply God's wisdom to their daily lives. In the Old Testament, proverbs were originally learned and shared from "generation to generation" (Psalm 78) orally, and later in written scriptures. In the Middle Ages, the Bible was translated into the language of the people and mass-produced on Johannes Gutenberg's printing press and widely disseminated. Today we can use the best of ancient proverbial wisdom, holistic learning methods, and digital technology to share the faith.

This book offers 50 carefully chosen biblical phrases or proverbs, which capture essential teachings of the Christian faith. Each phrase will be accompanied by a short reflection, questions to ponder, and age-appropriate learning activities and practices. Head, heart, and hands will involve the whole person in the learning process. This book can be used in a variety of settings: family devotions, Sunday school, confirmation, classes, retreats, and personal devotions. Use it over the course of a year of 50 weeks or pick those passages that speak most powerfully to your situation. Don't be in a hurry—read, reflect, pray, act and let God guide your steps.

> *Hold on to instruction, do not let it go, guard it well, for it is your life.*
> Proverbs 4:13

> *My child, pay attention to what I say, Turn your ear to my words. Do not let them out of your sight. Keep them in your heart. For they are life to those who find them and health to one's whole body.*
> Proverbs 4:20-22 (New Living Translation)

A Backpack to Have on Hand

There are many activities throughout this book that require a few basic supplies. Having these supplies in a small backpack in the classroom or the family closet ready at any moment will make this guide more useful and handy. Needed items: crayons, pencils, pens, markers, plain white copy paper, post-it notes, note cards, scissors, glue sticks, tape, yarn/string, dirt, seeds, paper cups, water, small bowls, hole punch, stapler, blindfold, chalk, and, of course, a bible. There may be more items specific to each activity, so read ahead to prepare. The short reflections are written with a high school youth and adult in mind. Adults, parents and youth leaders are encouraged to simplify and shorten the reflection with illustrations for your own life when the audience is children. To enrich your biblical understanding and enhance "youth-friendliness" encourage teens to use a bible phone app. Other helpful apps that can be downloaded to your smart phone include: Evernote (for journaling), Compass (for directions), Daily Verse (for meditation/devotions), Pinterest (for pics), You Tube (for short video clips).

A Cautionary Note

My friends, I beg you to listen as I teach. I will give explanation and explain the mystery of what happened long ago. These are things we learned from our ancestors and we will tell them to the next generation. We won't keep secret the glorious deeds and the mighty miracles of the Lord.
PSALM 78:1-4

While the focus of this book is proverbial wisdom or God sound bytes, it is important to keep in mind the context of these nuggets or pearls of wisdom. They are a part of a much larger story of God's choosing, teaching, chastening, and ultimately redeeming a people. This grand narrative is like the strand or string which holds all the gems of a necklace in place. The strand which holds it all together is love itself. On that strand are stories of God's glorious deeds and mighty miracles which people of faith have shared from "generation to generation." Telling these stories is a vital way of learning about God, the meaning of life, and how we are to live as humans. As these God stories are told we find our place in them and in the larger story of God's love. As we find our place in that story we write our own chapters in the God's unfolding story for the redemption of the whole creation. As we examine the smaller nuggets of biblical wisdom in this book we need to always remember their place within the story.

He used stories to teach them many things . . .
MARK 3: 2 (CONTEMPORARY ENGLISH VERSION)

It's not surprising that Jesus would use stories or parables as a primary way to teach his disciples. These parables of the kingdom were earthy stories taken from everyday life that taught about heavenly things and shared how God's reign was beginning in Jesus "on earth as in heaven." His stories were about seeds and soil, farming and fishing, food and festivals, money and taxes. These stories within the story make real and relevant God's love and mercy. Far from being fanciful fables, they are truth tales that we need to share, ponder, and apply to our lives today. Throughout the Old and

New Testaments, story is a fundamental way the faith is passed on and wisdom shared.

> *For by grace you are saved through faith and that not of yourselves; it is a gift of God; not as a result of works, that no one should boast.*
> EPHESIANS 2:8-9

When we focus on proverbial wisdom it is important to make a crucial theological distinction between law and gospel. God gave us the 10 Commandments (law) as a guide for life. The Bible describes and human history clearly demonstrates that we humans cannot keep the law. Quite to the contrary, human sinfulness (selfishness) has led to much brokenness, bloodshed, and bondage throughout time.

And so in the "fullness of time" (Galatians 4:4) God sent Jesus to save and redeem the world. This "good news" (gospel) is captured well in the words of the famous hymn: "Amazing grace how sweet the sound that saved a wretch like me. I once was lost, but now am found, was blind but now I see." The potential danger in a book focusing on proverbial wisdom or God sound bytes is that we might think if we memorize these passages, reflect on them, and apply them to our lives that we are then saved by our efforts. We need to remember that salvation is God's work and our grateful response to God's love in Jesus Christ is to humbly apply the wisdom of scripture to our daily lives. The law has three functions: to curb, to mirror, and to guide. The proverbial wisdom we will explore in this book holds the same potential value. But it doesn't save us!

Teaching and Learning Tip

God is Good…all the time…All the time…God is good!

Fresh out of seminary I was blessed to serve a small African American congregation in Connecticut. As is often the case with young pastors, I learned far more from the congregation I served than they learned from me. Whether in church or on the street a common greeting began "God is good!" to which the person being greeted would respond "All the time!" The original greeter would then say once again, with feeling, "God is good!" I later came to learn that this manner of greeting is sometimes described as "call and response" and was a common way to share greetings, to encourage one another, to teach, and to learn in the African American community.

As I reflected on that expression I remembered that in my Lutheran tradition the pastor begins worship with "The Lord be with you." And without prompting the congregation replies "And also with you." From the Middle Ages onward, European Christians called this pattern of response: antiphon or responsory. In Indian music this practice is known as *jugalbondi*. Whatever the tradition, this basic method of a simple repeated greeting and response has a venerated history as an effective way to teach and learn and form faith.

The danger with common expressions frequently repeated is that we don't mean what we say, as in "Hi, how are you?" "Fine thanks, how are you?" But I would contend that this kind of call and response approach to familiar proverbial expressions provides a wonderful opportunity to share God's wisdom! When I begin many of my classes I light a candle (remember 20-40-60-80) and say "Jesus Christ is the light of the world" to which my students learn to respond, "The light which no darkness can overcome!" With each candle lit and biblical expression shared, God's word becomes a "light to our path." Let's begin.

Day 1

In the beginning…God created the heavens and the earth.
Genesis 1:1

The main point of this passage and of the Creation Story in general is not to answer the question of how life began. A professor during my freshman year in college helped me understand that Genesis 1 is not science which asks how but it is theology which asks the question of who and why? Science is still trying to figure out the how question and there are many intriguing theories worth exploring using all the tools God gave us when we were created. The Creation Story shares our ancient ancestors deep theological conviction that "In the beginning…God created the heavens and the earth (Genesis 1:1)." So what difference does that make? It makes all the difference in the world because we learn in the rest of the story that God delights in the creation repeatedly announcing."It is good… very good." God creates a good place, a beautiful garden, in which we humans have all that we need for life including a relationship with God, the creator, the master gardener. God loves us so much that God entrusts to us the care of the earth. Why are we humans here? We are here to care for the creation, each other, and the God who gave us everything. We now can join in writing, and living, and telling the story. And it starts with "In the beginning . . . God created the heavens and the earth (Genesis 1:1)."

Reflection Questions:
- In what ways can I care for creation?
- What chapter would you like to add to God's story?

In the beginning… God created the heavens and the earth. Genesis 1:1

_____

_____

_____

_____

_____

_____

_____

_____

_____

_____

_____

_____

_____

Family Activity:

Using crayons, markers, paper and pictures, create a short family history. Each family member creates a page with his or her chapter.

Or go for a family "creation walk' and notice all the amazing things that God has created giving thanks as you go.

Teenage Activity:

Using your smart phone, create a photo album with the theme "God created . . ."

Adult Activity:

Draw a family tree on a large piece of paper using crayons, markers and pictures. Roots are your ancestors branches are your family of origin—fruit are your offspring.

Prayer:

In the beginning, God you blessed (me, our family, or us) with/ by . . .

Day 2

You shall love the Lord your God with your heart, soul, and strength . . . and you shall love your neighbor as yourself.
MARK 12:30-31

This is the answer Jesus gives to the Pharisees when they ask "What is the greatest commandment?" His answer actually isn't one of the 10 Commandments, but comes from the Shema, the prayer faithful Jews pray to begin and close each day."Hear, O Israel, the Lord your God is One, and you shall love the Lord with all your heart, soul, and strength and you shall teach these things to your children" (Deuteronomy 6: 4-7). Notice that Jesus has added "and you shall love your neighbor as yourself" (Mark 12:31). Why? Because if our love of God doesn't lead to caring for the people around us, then what's the point? One of my teachers warned of this danger when he said "We can become so heavenly-minded, we are no earthly good." The Old Testament prophets repeatedly called Israel to practice what they preached. Amos cried out "I hate your feasts and solemn assemblies, but let justice roll down like waters and righteousness like an ever flowing stream" (Amos 5:24). In his epistle, James, says "faith without works is dead." How will we finally be judged? Jesus answers, "When you do it for least of these you do it for me!" (Matthew 25:40) To be a Christian, a follower of Jesus, means to love God AND to love our neighbor!

Reflection Questions:
- How do you know others love you? Be specific.
- How do you show love to others? Give an example.
- Describe a recent example of how you loved a "neighbor."

_____

_____

_____

_____

_____

_____

_____

_____

_____

_____

_____

_____

_____

_____

_____

_____

> You shall love the Lord your God with your heart, soul, and strength... and you shall love your neighbor as yourself.
> Mark 12:30-31

Family Activity:
Cut out a large heart and write the word "LOVE" On the other side glue photos, objects or draw pictures of all those we are called to love (family, friends, community, world)

Teenage Activity:
Write a letter to a person who has made a positive impression on your life, explaining what they did and why it was meaningful to you. Be sure to give or send it. [Email]

Adult Activity:
Write a thank you note or letter to a person that has impacted your life.

Prayer:
Lord, help me/us to be thankful for the gift of love, which you have supplied and made alive in each of us. Help me/us to live out this gift of love to/by . . .

Day 3

We love . . . because God first loved us.
1 JOHN 4:19

This important passage is about "motivation." There are many motives or reasons why we humans do what we do. The Genesis story of creation begins with God's good creation, but ends with Adam and Eve's choice to put themselves before their creator. Putting one's self first is "sin." No wonder that the first commandment is "You shall have no other gods . . ." (Exodus 20:3). God's design for creation is to love God first and to love your neighbor as yourself. Notice the order: Love God first, Neighbor second, Self third. Unfortunately much of human history (wars, poverty, etc.) is motivated by human selfishness and greed, as we put "self" first. God's first great act of love was creation. We humans "live, because God gave us life." His second great act of love was giving to his people a set of rules or laws, the 10 Commandments, Why? "That you might have life." But sin and selfishness persisted, despite the warnings from prophetic messengers that God sent. So in the "fullness of time" God sent his son, Jesus, to save us from our sin and restore the good creation. In his life, death, and resurrection, God's love is perfected and made manifest in Jesus. Our salvation is based not on our following the rules or the law, but on God's grace, which we simply need to accept in faith as a gift. Why do we love? Because God first loved us!

Reflection Questions:
- How do you know that God loves you?
- Where do you struggle to show love?

We love...
because God
first loved us.
1 John 4:19

....

....

....

....

....

....

....

....

....

....

....

....

....

....

....

Family Activity:

Cut out hearts the size of a hand and add a ribbon trimming to the bottom to make an "award." Write in the middle "1st Loved by God." Take your special heart award and give it to someone.

Teenage Activity:

Write "I am loved . . ." on a post-it note and place on your mirror to remind you of God's love. Or write "I love you . . ." and leave for someone who needs to hear that good news.

Adult Activity:

Write, draw or photograph where you have witnessed God's love in the world today and imagine where you can share that love today in one specific way.

Prayer:

Thank you God for your perfect love. Help me/us to be aware of the "unloved" and be mindful, heartfelt, and moved to action to love…

Day 4

Repent . . . for the kingdom of God is at hand/near.
Matthew 4:17

When we realize that sin or selfishness/self-centeredness is the problem/illness, repentance is the first step in our recovery. This was John the Baptist's message in the wilderness, "Repent!" (Matthew 3:2). Centuries earlier the prophet Isaiah proclaimed "a voice crying in the wilderness, 'prepare the way of the Lord'" (Isaiah 40:3). Repentance begins with acknowledging and confessing our sinful condition. We accept the diagnosis of our dis-ease. But then we "turn around" (the Greek word is *metanoia* for repentance) and face in a new direction and begin a journey down a road away from ourselves toward loving God and our neighbor. I remember reading a book by psychologist Karl Menninger called *What Ever Became of Sin?* The book's thesis was that in modern times, many people would minimize the power or even deny the existence of sin. Some would say the problem is ignorance or lack of education, while others would suggest the problem is genetics or a lack of intelligence. While these issues may contribute to the world's problems, they don't explain or address the basic brokenness of humanity. Without this accurate diagnosis we simply may be putting a bandaid over a cancerous condition. Repentance is the radical first step of admitting our role in the problem and turning toward God who has the ultimate solution.

Reflection Questions:
- What are you hanging onto that weighs you down? Anger, hurt, fear?
- How can you let go, release, with God's help?

Repent...for
the kingdom
of God is at
hand/near.
Matthew 4:17

....

....

....

....

....

....

....

Family Activity:
Everyone makes a fist and holds it tight for a whole minute. Now release it. Many times we hold onto our sin (anger, hurt, fear) not willing to ask for forgiveness or help. Reflect on how tiring it is to hold onto a tight fist (sins).

Teenage Activity:
Place three rocks in your backpack that represent things you are holding onto. Travel with those for a whole week everywhere you go. Reflect on how tiring it is, and how it feels to remove them at the week's end.

Or practice the Jesus Prayer/Prayer of the Heart by slowly repeating for several minutes the phrase "Lord Jesus have mercy on me."

Adult Activity:
Write down on a piece of paper things you are holding onto. Shred the paper and soak the remnants in a bowl of water to make paper mulch. Place the paper mulch onto a paper bag, using it as a make-shift strainer. Add flat flower seeds to your paper mulch as it is patted flat. When it is dry you can plant the paper and flowers will grow. Share them with someone!

Prayer:
God, I confess that I am far from perfect and I struggle daily with sin that tempts me to drift away from your forgiveness and love. Grant your forgiveness and release from the burden of my sins and help me forgive…

Day 5

Do onto others . . . as you would have them do unto you.
Matthew 7:12

I think this is the first verse from the Bible I knew "by heart." The passage was drilled into me by my mom. Given that I was a "handful" (her words) I suspect I needed to hear this passage repeatedly. Now, many years later, I can still remember that when I first heard it, it made me pause (briefly) and think. Even though I was a child, who wanted to play with other kid's toys, it made sense in a very rudimentary way, that I should treat my sister's stuff well, because I expected her to take good care of my toys. Maybe the common sense-ness of the "golden rule" is why this verse has counterparts in many of the great religions of the world. Confucius said "What you do not wish for yourself, do not do to other," and Islam teaches, "That which you want for yourself, seek for mankind." In many ways the Golden Rule is a kind of common sense which is the essential ethical foundation for a healthy human community. But, to quote my dad, it is "easier said than done." Maybe the Apostle Paul said it best "That which I would do, I do not; and that which would not do, I do" (Romans 7:19). Or perhaps "All sin . . . and fall short of the glory of God" (Romans 3:23). The rule is still golden and worthy of our best efforts even though we tarnish it on a regular basis.

Reflection Questions:
- How do you feel when you are treated unfairly?
- What do you to treat others fairly?

....
....
....
....
....
....
....
....
....
....
....

Family Activity:

Everyone take turns and share one thing that you wish everyone would do for each other in your home and in the world.
What are the similarities? How can you begin living more harmoniously? What areas do you need to change? Everyone pick
one of your items and come up with a plan on how to support
each other in doing it.

Teenage Activity:

Give some examples of the Golden Rule in action with your
friends at school. Make a list of things that happen with your
friends that are in conflict with the Golden Rule. How can
you become a positive influence with your friends by your
example?

Adult Activity:

How does the Golden Rule impact your daily life? Are there
days when following it seems more difficult or easier? Do you
find that most people follow the Golden Rule? Choose one
specific thing you can do to live the Golden Rule. Live it.

Prayer:

Lord, help me to live more harmoniously in your kingdom by . . .

Day 6

And now these three remain: faith, hope, and love . . . but the greatest of these is love.
1 CORINTHIANS 13:13

We all know this one, right? I have to confess that I really don't like it. Perhaps it's better to say I'm tired of hearing it, as being a pastor I've been asked countless times to preach on this passage at weddings. I suspect I have preached on "the greatest of these is love" more than any other passage in the Bible. Yes, "familiarity breeds contempt" (Mark Twain), but maybe my struggle is that the message was originally intended for the larger faith community and not couples getting married. The message to the whole Christian community is simple: Faith and hope are important gifts but unless they are motivated by and shared with and through love, they have no value or may even be negative like a "noisy gong or a clanging symbol" (1 Corinthians 13:1). Faith can "move mountains" and hope can "endure all things" but without love each is too often about me and not the other, the neighbor, the community. We love, because God first loved us. In other words, the gift of God's love is exactly that, a gift which is to be shared with others and for others.

Reflection Questions:
- How do you or where have you witnessed God's love in the world? In your life?
- Where have you re-gifted God's gift of love to others?
- When you first think of the word "love", do you think first of those who have impacted and loved you, or do you think of those you love or have loved?

> And now these three remain: faith, hope, and love...but the greatest of these is love.
> 1 Corinthians 13:13

Family Activity:

Discuss what you feel the difference is between faith, hope and love. Why is love the most important? Write the words "love" "hope" and "faith" on square pieces of paper. Decorate them to look like a wrapped present. Post them where everyone can see them every day. When guests ask, share what you have reflected upon.

Teenage Activity:

Make the word "love" your screen saver (great images on Pinterest) Remember: you have that same gift of love to re-gift to others. You choose how every day.

Adult Activity:

Reflect on faith, hope and love and how they impact your life. Why do you think love is the greatest? How does love of your community and neighbor impact your life? Finish this phrase and how it applies in your life: "Love is…" Keep it handy so that you can regularly reflect and act on it.

Prayer:

Lord, may I not be a noisy gong or a clanging symbol, but help me to grow in your gift of love and to re-gift it to your world by . . .

Day 7

One does not live by bread alone . . . but by every word that comes from the mouth of the Lord.
DEUTERONOMY 8:3

We have heard this passage so often perhaps we might say, "Duh!" Or maybe we think this is a reminder to go to church or to read our bibles. While each reaction is understandable and contains an element of truth, this well-known verse has far more wisdom to share when we examine its context. God has given Israel the 10 Commandments not just that they might avoid problems but that they "might have life."

Deuteronomy tell us that "the Lord your God has led you these forty years in the wilderness, in order to humble you, testing you to know what was in your heart, whether or not you would keep his commandments. He humbled you by letting you hunger, then by feeding you with manna…in order that you understand that one does not live by bread alone but by every word that comes from the mouth of the Lord (Matthew 4:4)." In the "Wilderness School" as theologian and author Dan Erlander calls it, the Hebrew people came to understand that in addition to bread, they were totally dependent upon God for life itself. They were about to leave the desert and enter the Promised Land, a land flowing in milk and honey. In their new-found prosperity they would soon be tempted to forget the source of all their blessings and place themselves rather than God at the center of their universe. For those of us who live in the richest nation on earth, this couldn't be a more timely and humbling reminder!

Reflection Questions:
- How do you "think" about food?
- What does it mean to be humbled by "letting you hunger?"

_____

_____

_____

_____

_____

_____

_____

_____

_____

_____

_____

_____

_____

_____

> One does not live by bread alone...but by every word that comes from the mouth of the Lord. Deuteronomy 8:3

Family Activity:

If you have excess food in your cupboard, box it up and take it to the food bank or where food donations are accepted and slip a note card with today's bible verse in with the food to be shared with others.

Teenage Activity:

Take time to research a local feeding program in your area. Become a volunteer. Become the hands that feed. By allowing God to work his wonders through you- you too shall be fed! Commit to feeding yourself daily with God's word by adding a Bible app to your smart phone and reading one verse a day.

Adult Activity:

Add a Bible app to your smart phone and read/ponder a verse a day!

Prayer:

Lord, you made this earth with enough to feed all your people. Feed us with your word that we might feed a hungry world…

Day 8

In the beginning was the Word . . . and the word became flesh.
JOHN 1:1 AND 14

In the beginning God spoke a creative "word" and all that we know—oceans, birds, trees, stars, and humans—came into existence. God's "word" created everything from the tiny amoeba to the vast universe. Like the Psalmist, my response to this vast cosmic image is: "When I look at your heavens, the work of your fingers, the moon and the stars that you have established, what are human beings that you are mindful of them, mortals that you care for them?"(Psalm 8:3) But read more carefully. That word or *logos* was "with God." That "word was God." John's version of the Good News begins with this vast cosmic image created by God's word. And here's the best part, "The Word became flesh and lived among us" (John 1:14). That word that was in the beginning creating everything has come in human form to live with us humans to demonstrate how much God cares for and loves us. A little boy invited his friend to come to Sunday School with him. After class, the boy's friend asked who Jesus really was."Well, Jesus is God with flesh on." The same God whose vast creation staggers our imagination enters into the creation as a human being in Jesus. And the God who said "let there be light"(Genesis 1:3) is also in Jesus the "true light, which enlightens everyone, was coming into the world" (John 1:9). May this living Word be a light to our paths!

Reflection Questions:
- Have you ever been lost in the dark (figuratively or literally)?
- Who has been God's light for you?

_____

_____

_____

_____

_____

_____

_____

_____

_____

_____

In the beginning was the Word...and the word became flesh. John 1:1, 14

Family Activity:

Take turns being blindfolded and told to find an object or room in the house without help. How difficult is it? Now re-move the blindfold and do the task. We falter when we can't see what we are doing or where we are going. However, with Jesus as our light, we aren't in the darkness anymore and all things are possible.

Teenage Activity:

Take a walk after dark and pay attention to your thoughts and feelings. Turn on your flashlight (light of smart/cell phone) and notice how the light changes everything. With the help of the light, write down the ways Christ gives direction to your life. (You can use the Evernote app to do so.)

Adult Activity:

Think of a dark or confusing place in your life where you need the light of Christ and invite a trusted Christian friend to help you find your way.

Prayer:

Lord, thank you for being my dependable light in this world. Help me to follow you and not stumble in the darkness over . . .

Day 9

Take up your cross . . . and follow me!
LUKE 9:23

What does "discipleship" mean? Jesus said, "If anyone would come after me, then he must deny himself and daily take up his cross and follow me."

Notice first that being a disciple of Jesus is more than believing. Yes, one is to "believe on the Lord Jesus Christ, and you will be saved." But belief is more than "agreeing" with or assenting to a set of doctrines or principles. It takes a deeper commitment than simply admiring Jesus' teachings. There are three steps: 1. Deny oneself: This means replacing "me" and putting Jesus at the center of one's life. Because we confess that we are sinful this will challenge our basic instincts for self-gratification as humans. 2. Take up your cross, daily: The cross of Jesus is not the annoying and petty problems we face as human beings. The cross we are to take up is about dying to ourselves and living for God and others which will by its very nature be counter-cultural. Notice that this is not a one-time decision but as Martin Luther reminds us, a daily dying and rising with Christ and a life-time journey of faith. 3. Finally, follow me: Just as Jesus' disciples long ago followed their rabbi/teacher, our discipleship today is a daily following of Jesus as he leads, guides, and directs our lives. That journey will involve suffering and pain—count on it—but it will also bring deep joy and peace knowing God is using us to bring about his kingdom.

Reflection Questions:
- What does it mean to you to put Jesus at the center of your life? To deny yourself?
- Can you think of a time recently when you took up your cross and followed?

....

....

....

....

....

....

....

....

Take up your cross...and follow me! Luke 9:23

Family Activity:

Think of something that you can do to follow Jesus and care for others. Are there toys or other household items that are no longer used? Gather them and deliver them to a homeless shelter or save all your change for the week and donate it to help the needy. Is there something that you can volunteer to do at your church?

Teenage Activity:

Living for God and others can mean making choices. Ask God for direction on how you can serve him today. Is there someone who needs your help or prayer? Activate the Compass or add as an app on your smart phone—use it as a reminder to ask God for direction.

Or find a cross in your home and take 5 minutes to quietly meditate on God's costly love.

Adult Activity:

Think about where you see God at work in your life. How is God leading you to serve him? List your gifts, passions and abilities. How could you use those to serve others in your church or in the community?

Prayer:

Lord Jesus you have asked me to take up my cross and follow you. I need your guidance. Guide me in . . .

Day 10

I have come that you might have life . . . and have it abundantly.
JOHN 10:10

The Christian faith is often portrayed in very negative terms: When I was a boy, one of the messages I heard was Christians shouldn't "smoke, drink, dance, or play cards." Sound familiar? As a result my impression of many religious people was a pretty serious, pious, somber, even sour bunch. Who would want to be a part of that club, I wondered? Then I discovered a passage in John's Gospel which gave me a more positive, hopeful, and inviting vision of why Jesus came to earth."I have come that you might have life . . . and have it more abundantly." Jesus has just described himself as the good shepherd and, like a shepherd; Jesus protects us from the dangers of the world. But his ultimate goal is to lead us to abundant and full life. Do you hear the echo of Psalm 23: "The Lord is my shepherd, I shall not want. He makes me lie down in green pastures, he leads me beside still waters, he restores my soul" (Psalm 23:1-2). We cannot deny or ignore the temptations or problems in our lives and in the world. But God's ultimate hope for creation is renewal and restoration. God's kingdom which has begun to dawn in Jesus, is a world where God's abundant blessings are generously shared with all people for sake of the whole creation.

Reflection Questions:
- Jesus said, "I have come that you might have life . . . and have it abundantly" (John 10:10). What does this mean to you?
- What are the things that give you the most joy and satisfaction? (material item or relational?)

....

....

....

....

....

....

....

....

....

....

....

....

....

I have come that you might have life...and have it abundantly. John 10:10

Family Activity:

Create a family "abundance" list (strengths/assets) and write a short (3 sentences) family pledge with ways your family can share of its abundance of time, money, prayer, or service with others.

Teenage Activity:

Life is wonderful when you feel that you "fit in", but sometimes we don't feel like we do. Too fat, too skinny, too shy, not smart enough—we all have lots of doubts about ourselves and need the reassurance that we're okay. Text or email a word of encouragement to someone who needs it!

Adult Activity:

Take a moment to think about what gives meaning to your life. Are they things or moments of care and love? What can you do to share the love and care that Jesus gives at home, community and world?

Prayer:

Lord Jesus, help me to . . .

Day 11

Remember the Sabbath day to keep it holy.
Exodus 20:8

The 4th Commandment is often interpreted as "Go to church."

Judging by church attendance figures in recent years, this teaching isn't working. In the Northwest, fewer than 20% of the population goes to church. In the more "religious" Midwest, it's close to 50%. Going to church certainly is one way to "remember the Sabbath," but that wasn't the original and deep intention of the commandment. On the Sabbath (the seventh day in the creation story), "God rested and beheld all that he had created and declared, 'It is good....very good'." The Sabbath originally was a day to rest from our labors and celebrate the goodness of the creator and the creation. Abraham Heschel, a noted Jewish scholar, in his wonderful little book, *The Sabbath*, says the Sabbath should not focus on simply recovering from or preparing for the work in our week. Rather it should be a time to savor and enjoy the gift of life itself. Sabbath should be the crown not the caboose of creation. Despite labor-saving devices, vacations, and leaves of various sorts, we are busier and more stressed than ever. McDonald's understood our human need for rest when they coined the phrase, "You deserve a break today!" Resting is hard for some of us type A personalities. It takes practice, but it's worth it. Long before health experts extolled the virtues of rest, God suggested—no, commanded—we take time to rest. Try it . . . you'll like it!

Reflection Questions:
- What brings you stress or makes you tired?
- How do you relax? What brings you Sabbath/rest?

Remember
the Sabbath
day to keep it
holy.
Exodus 20:8

....

....

....

....

....

....

....

....

....

....

....

Family Activity:

Talk about and decide on a family "Sabbath" (day, half-day) and what it will look like. Make it happen and make it a habit.

Teenage Activity:

Create a mini-sabbath each week (day or half day or hour) when you turn off electronics and use that free time to pray, go for a walk, have a needed conversation, take a nap.

Adult Activity:

Choose a time to stop and reflect on the goodness of your week's work. Review your accomplishments. Don't make a list of the unfinished tasks, as this is easy to do, but honestly reflect on at least three items that you feel you have done well or that God has done in the week. It's always easy to say what you need to still do, but harder to say, "Look at what I did this week. It is good. Very good!" Enjoy your Sabbath.

Prayer:

Lord, even you rested on the seventh day and commanded and gave the important example of Sabbath, I/we often get caught up in the busy demands of this world. Help me/us to rest by allowing me/us to . . .

Day 12

Be still . . . and know that I am God.
PSALM 46:10

"Sit still!" I can still hear my mother's voice from when I was a little boy. My grandmother's expression was "you have ants in your pants." And she was right: I couldn't sit in one place for long; it's still a challenge for this Type A personality. I resonate to a book title I heard of a number of years ago, *When I Sit I Feel Guilty*. I didn't sit long enough to read it. I don't think, however, this passage's intent is make children or adults feel guilty as they actively live out their faith. Rather it is a strong reminder that from time to time and on a regular basis we need to quiet all the voices clamoring for our attention, empty ourselves, and listen for God's voice. Psalm 46 speaks of the many ways God is present: God is a "very present help in trouble" who even "makes wars to cease." But if we are too busy and not paying attention we don't realize that "The Lord of hosts is with us; the God of Jacob is our refuge." God wants all children to know he is with us to help us, to be our refuge and strength . . . and God's voice sounds remarkably like my mom's. Thanks be to God!

Reflection Questions:
- Do you find peace in being still? Or is being still difficult?
- Where do find the calm and quiet needed to hear God's voice for direction?

Family Activity:

Play a game: dance around and make noise, then have a leader shout "Be still!" and everyone else responds "and know that I am God" while freezing in whatever position they are in. Do a couple rounds of this, taking turns leading. Try it without any noise, but just actions. Is it easier to hear the leader say "Be still"? Does the leader even have to raise his/her voice? Can the leader still have everyone stop even with a whisper? God usually doesn't shout for our attention. It comes in a small still voice, even a whisper. Have everyone hold hands and calmly inhale saying "be still" and then exhale saying, "and know that I am God." With each breath drop one word from the end of the phrase.

Teenage Activity:

It's easy to get frazzled and disoriented when life is busy and things don't go as planned. When times of trouble and stress come upon you, have faith that God is there. Be still, and know that God is there. Do a breathing exercise by inhaling "Be still" and then exhaling the phrase "and know that I am God." Say this quietly to yourself, inhaling and exhaling, each time dropping one word off the end of the phrase.

Adult Activity:

Take a deep breath. Repeat the phrase "Be still and know that I am God." Repeat this each time exhaling "Be still" and inhaling "and know that I am God." With each cycle, decrease the phrase by one word. This breathing exercise will bring calm and focus. The last cycles of this exercise will help you to "be still" and simply "be" in God's presence.

Prayer:

Lord, you provide the very breath I breathe. Help me to better know your presence in my busy life. Help me to . . .

Be still...and know that I am God.
Psalm 46:10

Day 13

Speaking the truth . . . in love.
EPHESIANS 4:15

We all aspire to be truthful and loving, right? We all, as children, learned to never tell a lie and to love each other. But here the two are joined together. Why? I think it's because we often do one or the other: we speak the truth, but in an unloving way and hurt someone in the process. Or, we sugar-coat a situation in an attempt to be loving and we don't really tell the truth. It's hard to keep the two together and to keep them in tension. This kind of teaching is common in the Bible and used frequently by Jesus. Here, the Apostle Paul is teaching the young church at Ephesus about the importance of unity in the body of Christ. Just as each part of a human body is important to overall health, each member is valuable to the health of the church. All those body parts are connected by ligaments and tendons which hold the body together. Without them the body would fall apart. Speaking the truth in love is like those tendons and ligaments which hold the church together. Truth without love is inflexible and brittle. Love without truth has no backbone or structure. We live in that creative tension. We are frequently faced with situations where we would be wise to pause, reflect, pray for guidance, and then "speak the truth in love."

Reflection Questions:
- When was the last time you reacted to a situation with outright uncensored honesty?
- What happened the last time you spoke with love, but not truth, only for the truth to come out later?
- What does living in the tension of love and truth mean to you?

Speaking the
truth...in love.
Ephesians
4:15

....

....

....

....

....

....

....

....

....

....

Family Activity

Stand in a circle with your toes all touching, then take a step back. While holding hands, continue taking steps back until you are stretched to the limit. Now lean back, making the connection of hands be the support of the circle's weight. When one person isn't balanced in their care for the group, it affects everyone and how they respond to the shift in weight and pull. Tension is good, but uneven tension causes us to fall and to break apart.

Teenage Activity:

Think of the last time you spoke without reflecting. Did it harm someone? How could you have dealt with the situation differently? Practice pausing and attempting to see all angles of the situation you are facing which requires telling the truth in a loving manner.

Adult Activity:

Words matter. Think of a situation where you need to speak the truth in love. Write out a script for what you need to say. Practice, pray, and try it.

Prayer:

Dear God, I trust you and give thanks and praise to you for the words of care and life you give to me. Help me to speak the truth in love to . . .

Day 14

Be angry . . . but do not sin.
EPHESIANS 4:26

I remember as a child being told, "Don't be angry! Be nice!" While well-intended, this advice often conveys the message that anger is bad and that we should "stuff" that feeling. Anger, however, is a normal human emotion which we experience. This passage affirms the honest emotion of anger with a caveat, "but do not sin." In other words, it is important and even healthy to express one's feelings. But we should be aware of how sharing our feelings affects others so that we don't sin. What does this mean? The essence of sin is selfishness, so if our expression of anger is "just about me" and is simply venting without regard to the other, we have sinned. And often our outburst makes the problem worse and provokes anger in the other person. The passage goes on to say "do not let the sun go down on your anger." Unexpressed anger has a way of smoldering and hurting both the angry person and those around him/her. Paul writes to the Corinthians, "Love does not keep a record of wrongs" (1 Corinthians 13:6). Instead of stuffing the anger, we are encouraged to share it in a loving and sensitive way and in the process we can begin to wipe the slate clean. Just as God has forgiven us, we can share that forgiveness with others.

Reflection Questions:
- What was the last situation you were angry over?
- Do you feel guilty or still angry over the situation? Why or why not?

Family Activity:

Take a piece of paper and on one half draw a picture that symbolizes a time when you were angry. What colors do you use? What forms do you use? By drawing this scene, does it bring back the emotion of anger? Now on the other half draw a picture of God loving you. What does this look like? What colors did you use now? Post your pictures on the refrigerator to remind you how God can help you "be angry but not sin."

Be angry...but do not sin. Ephesians 4:26

Teenage Activity:

Hold onto a pencil in your hand making a fist. This fist represents the steps that must be taken to forgive and let go of the anger in a healthy and responsible way. Anger is represented by the pencil. Lift up your thumb; this represents remembering what you are angry about. Lift up your pointer finger; this represents naming the person(s) who have contributed to your anger. The pencil is probably getting harder to hold onto. Lift up your index finger; admit your anger and name it. Next lift up your ring finger; remember the promises made by God to you—you are forgiven—you are called upon to forgive others. Finally, let go of your anger so you can use your hand. Lift up your pinky finger; pray for God's guidance and strength to take your anger and help turn it into love for your enemy, maybe even love for yourself. When you let go of your anger you can be God's hands in the world.

Adult Activity:

Take five minutes and look into the mirror, reflecting on an issue that is causing you anger. Say out loud "I am angry because…" Remember the promise God's gives in Jesus Christ to us that we are forgiven and must forgive others. Pray for God's spirit to help release your anger and forgive another.

Prayer:

Lord Jesus, you have forgiven me and shown me grace and love despite my numerous faults. Guide me to love and forgive . . .

Day 15

Come to me all who are weary and are heavily burdened . . . and I will give you rest.
Matthew 11:28

Recently one of my adult children stopped by after a day of work at her new, first full-time job. She was exhausted. I had to bite my tongue and not blurt out, "Wait until you are married, have kids, and a job!" My younger college students often share how exhausted they are, and I have to confess I have said, "Wait until you enter the real world." Perhaps the best place to begin is to confess that we all experience weariness and frequently feel heavily burdened and that often it's our own choices that leave us exhausted. Whatever the cause, Jesus simply invites us all to come to him and he will give us rest. But there is more to the passage: "Take my yoke upon you and learn from me: for I am gentle and humble in heart, and you will find rest for your souls. For my yoke is easy and my burden is light" (Matthew 11:29). A yoke is the wooden piece which makes it possible for a heavy load to be shared equally by two animals. When we are yoked with Jesus, our load is lightened. This image is used in other places in the Bible to describe how a husband and wife are yoked together in marriage. But Jesus promises more than just a day off; he promises rest for your soul. Back to confession: Isn't much of our weariness driven by trying to impress others, to prove our worth, to maybe even earn our salvation? The soul-rest that Jesus provides is rooted in God's deep love for us. As we rest in that grace, we can be renewed and sent forth to love a weary and burdened world!

Reflection Questions:
- At what times do you feel weary?
- To what extent is your exhaustion from choices you have made? Why have you made these choices?

....

....

....

....

....

....

Come to me
all who are
weary and
are heavily
burdened...
and I will give
you rest.
Matthew
11:28

Family Activity:

Take a few moments to share what your perfect dream day of rest would be like. Partner up and take one arm each and lock it around each other's waist sideways, so you are standing side by side, but with only two arms exposed. Now attempt a task in the house or yard, such as pushing a wheelbarrow or filling a cup of water while holding it. It takes both of your hands to complete the task. Many hands make work easy and sharing our burdens with Jesus lightens the load.

Teenage Activity:

Pick up a heavy object like a cement block and carry it as far as you can. Invite someone to share the load and see how much farther you can carry it. How was the experience different? How does this lesson apply to my daily life? What can Christ help me carry? Who needs my help in carrying their load?

Adult Activity:

Draw a cross. Under each arm of the cross write your list of burdens. The load is not yours alone. Christ promises to lighten your burden by you taking on his yoke. His yoke is his love and ultimate sacrifice for you. You are not alone in these burdens. Find rest in knowing that Christ carries them side by side with you. He will never abandon you or leave you. He will always be there helping carry the load.

Prayer:

Lord Jesus, I often forget you during my busy and stressful days. Help me to believe and trust in your promise of rest in your yoke, and that you call me to help carry . . .

Day 16

A soft answer . . . turns away wrath.
PROVERBS 15:1

My mother taught junior high English. As I grew up I wondered how she did it. Unlike my junior high gym teacher who was tough, strong, and powerful, my mom was a small and gentle person who loved nothing more than reciting poetry. I figured a typical junior high class would eat her alive. When I asked her secret, she said, "The louder the students get, the quieter I speak." I was speechless."That's all there is to it?" I asked."Well, not quite," she said."I also love what I teach and I love the students, too." Maybe that's what this proverb about a "soft answer turning away wrath" might be hinting at. I am not advocating a soft answer in every situation, but think of the times when your answer was not heard because of your tone, volume, or spirit. Too often an angry response to another person's anger simply fuels the fire and the problem grows worse. A quiet response can have a calming effect, especially if it is motivated by love. My mom's motivation wasn't simply to calm down a rowdy classroom. She wanted to teach the subject she loved to students she cared deeply about. One of my teachers once said, "Kids have crap detectors." They can tell when we are "full of it." I think they can also tell when we really care. It won't always work, but I believe that over time a soft answer plus a healthy dose of God's love, will not only turn away wrath, it will bring real peace.

Reflection Questions:
- Where have you witnessed or felt love? Wrath?
- How do you react to a loud response verses a soft answer?

Family Activity:

On a note card write "God is with you, Child of God. God will always be with you. God loves you." Appoint a leader in the family to repeat the words on the card softly and calmly, without showing the other family members the words on the card. This person is to be the "soft answer." The rest of the family is to be the "wrath." The Wrath voices should be loud and noisy in their talking and actions. The leader continues to speak in a calm and soft voice. Continue this activity for 10 minutes or until the wrath-filled voices and actions run out of energy and want to know what the "soft answer" is saying. As a family reflect on your experience and possible life-applications.

Teenage Activity:

What are the issues that get you "worked up?" There are a lot of injustices in the world, and things aren't black and white or as easy as we once thought. Finding the ability to be the "soft answer" or even hear it can be very difficult. When in moments of wrath, (yours or another's) remember to pause, take a deep breath and release your tensed up muscles. Our hearing receptors are heightened when emotion is high which affects our ability to listen. Turn down the volume and speak quietly and peacefully with love.

Adult Activity:

Who or what makes you angry? Next time you find yourself in a moment of anger, take a deep breath and pause: Find calmness. Try to intently listen to what is really happening around you. Next time you find yourself in the middle of another's wrath, rather than reacting, become conscious of their need for calm. Help them by speaking softly in love. Both sides will be rewarded.

Prayer:

Lord, you speak to us in a soft still voice. Help me to practice speaking and answering in soft and loving ways. Help me in situations such as . . .

A soft answer...turns away wrath. Proverbs 15:1

Day 17

Sow the wind . . . reap the whirlwind.
HOSEA 8:7

I love to garden. My grandmother planted the seed (pardon the pun)! Grandma's garden was very organized: When we planted seeds, we stretched a string between two stakes and very carefully planted with proper spacing of carrots, beans, radishes, and corn. If I had been in charge I would have been a little more carefree and creative. It was only later that I heard the parable Jesus told about the sower (Mark 4) who gardened like I would by throwing seeds all over the place. What Grandma was teaching me is that how and where you plant seeds makes a difference when the plants begin to sprout. And that's what the Prophet Hosea is trying to teach God's people, "Sow the wind", "reap the whirlwind." He was reminding God's people that their careless lives (sowing seeds in windy conditions) and worshipping many gods would lead to destruction (a messy garden).

The seeds of our lives are a precious gift and God, who began it all with an amazing garden, wants our lives to be productive and fruitful."Reaping the whirlwind" also points to the reality that what may seem like a simple and small act can have huge consequences far beyond what we intended. Careful planning in our life-decisions (gardening) isn't meant to take the joy out of living, but to enhance the feast God invites us to enjoy and share with others.

Reflection Questions:
- What was the last thing you sowed or planted?
- What preparations did you make before planting?

Sow the
wind...
reap the
whirlwind.
Hosea 8:7

....

....

....

....

....

....

....

....

....

....

....

....

....

....

....

Family Activity:

Plan a garden together. It can be a small window or planter garden or the full size deal. Gather the necessary tools and supplies. Reflect during the planting, growing and harvesting seasons on what is happening in the garden and why it is happening. Notice the little changes.

Teenage Activity:

What's going well in your life? What's a struggle? What in your life is the result of careful planning? What in your life is chaotic and the result of a whirlwind approach? Write your thoughts in your journal (such as on Evernote).

Adult Activity:

Reflect on your garden of life: What has the whirlwind planted? Where have you been productive? What needs weeding or pruning or cultivating?

Prayer:

Creator Lord, you have sown your love in me. Help me to sow in my life and in this world . . .

Day 18

Bad company . . . corrupts good morals.
1 Corinthians 15:33

I can just hear my teenage daughter grunting "Duh!" as she rolls her eyes. The Apostle Paul's words of warning to the Christians at Corinth is echoed by generations of parents and teachers, "Don't hang out with the wrong crowd!" In *Poor Richard's Almanac*, Ben Franklin adapts a 14th century Latin proverb which we <u>all</u> can repeat from memory, "A rotten apple…spoils the whole barrel." As with many proverbs this sage advice has survived the test of time because it is true. If we hang out with bad company our morals will likely be corrupted. Paul was battling an "eat, drink, and be merry" philosophy (verse 32) based on the belief that when you die, that's the end; so "grab the gusto." Because our lives don't really matter, we can live with a "whatever" attitude. The new Christian philosophy proclaimed that those who die believing in Jesus Christ, will like him, be raised from the dead. Because Christ being was raised from the dead as the "first fruits of those who have died" (verse 20) our lives take on an eternal significance. How we live and who we hang out with are vitally important. But lest we turn this passage into an excuse to create a pious and private and perfect people, remember who Jesus hung out with sharing God's deep love for them: the poor, the widow, the sick, the sinners of his day. We are called to bring a new way of living and dying and rising to the whole world.

Reflection Questions:
- Who do you hang out with?
- Who are the top three people/groups that influence your daily living?

....

....

....

....

....

....

....

....

....

Bad company... corrupts good morals.
1 Corinthians 15:33

Family Activity:

Play the game of "Faces." Choose one person to share their excitement about going to the zoo (or whatever place they choose). The other family members are the "faces" we encounter and influence us. The "faces" are to reflect a particular attitude, such as angry versus happy. The sharing person spends 2 minutes trying to talk to the angry faces. Then 2 minutes talking to the happy faces. Was there a difference on how it made you feel interacting with each group of faces? Choose friends wisely, as they will influence you. Also remember that you have the power of influence, and you can make someone happy who is grumpy or sad.

Teenage Activity:

Take a magazine or look at a e-zine and identify what the positive and negative advertising "messages." Who are the good and bad influences in your life? Who and how do you influence others?

Adult Activity:

Reflect on where you've encountered influences in your life, good or bad. Where have you given influence others? Where can you be a positive influence?

Prayer:

Lord Jesus, you were the example for all to follow in how we should live our lives. Help me to . . .

Day 19

Forgive us our trespasses ... as we forgive those who
trespass against us.
Matthew 6:12

The Eagles' Don Henley sings, "I've been trying to get down to the heart of the matter but my will gets weak and my thoughts seem to scatter, but I think it's about forgiveness ... forgiveness, even if you don't love me anymore." I think he's right. In the middle of the prayer Jesus taught us to pray, we are to ask God to "forgive us ... as we forgive those who trespass against us." We know that God in Christ forgives us on the cross. The bigger challenge is our forgiving others who have trespassed against us. It's hard to forgive. Maybe the wound is so deep we can hardly function. Maybe our anger simply wants revenge. Or perhaps we nurse the wound and subtly punish the offender in more passive-aggressive ways. But Jesus and Don are right, this is the heart of the matter. This is the heart of the Christian faith: forgiveness. It must begin with confessing our own sins or trespasses which God graciously forgives. Certainly, others have sinned against me, but each of us has sinned in thought, word, and deed. We sing Psalm 51, "Create in me a clean heart, Oh God, and renew a right spirit within me." Whether our hearts are weighed down with guilt, anger, or pain, God promises the bypass surgery of forgiveness. It is still is often difficult to forgive, but it is the "heart of the matter" which brings healing to families, communities, and even the world.

Reflection Questions:
- What sin/transgression against you do you hold onto?
- What sin/transgression of your own do you need to ask forgiveness for?

....
....
....
....
....
....
....
....
....
....
....

> Forgive us our trespasses... as we forgive those who trespass against us.
> Matthew 6:12

Family Activity:

As a family imagine a situation and do a role play of what forgiveness might look like. Take role and try it out. Switch roles and repeat the exercise and discuss how you felt and what you learned. Practice during the week at home, school, and work.

Teenage Activity:

Imagine a person you need to forgive and use "centering prayer" to let God help you soften your heart. For 10 minutes in a quiet place with eyes closed imagine the person/situation needing forgiveness, a repeat every 10 seconds the phrase, "God forgive . . ."
Repeat this practice until you are ready to speak with the person a word of forgiveness.

Adult Activity:

Write a note of love or request of forgiveness to someone you know.

Prayer:

Dear Lord, I confess that I am not perfect and have held anger, guilt and shame too close to my heart. I have held onto another's sins, and have not granted forgiveness and peace between us. Help me to . . .

Day 20

It is more blessed to give . . . than to receive.
Acts 20:35

When did you first hear this phrase? Did one of your parents quote it when you refused to share a toy with your sister? Or was it in a sermon during the stewardship appeal at church? Whatever the setting, this phrase has become a part of the common language both inside and outside the church. The original context in Acts is the Apostle Paul teaching the elders at Ephesus before he sailed to Jerusalem. Clearly he is talking about money or material possessions. He says, "I coveted no one's silver or gold or clothing" (Acts 20:33). In fact Paul had supported himself as a "tentmaker" during his missionary journeys."In all this I have given you an example that by such work we must support the weak, remembering the words of the Lord Jesus, for he himself said, 'It is more blessed to give than to receive'." Two things stand out: Giving is a blessed thing to do and that giving is to support the weak. I think this wisdom is crystallized in the phrase "we are blessed to be a blessing" (2 Corinthians 8-9). Paul and Jesus are saying that because we are blessed we must share with others less fortunate and in that sharing both they and we are blessed. The Old Testament Prophets repeatedly call God's people to care for the weak and marginalized. James says it best, "Religion that is pure and undefiled before God, the Father, is this: to care for orphans and widows in their distress" (James 1: 27). As we share with the weak we join in proclaiming and bringing God's kingdom on earth as in heaven.

Reflection Questions:

- What was the last thing you received from another person?
- What was the last thing you gave to someone else?

It is more blessed to give...than to receive.
Acts 20:35

Family Activity:
Take three bowls and fill them half full of water. Have a towel ready. Take a cup and explain how when you give to another, it helps fill their bowl. Also, as one gives to us, our bowl becomes fuller. If everyone does both actions, we all are consistently filled and filling others. But what happens if the two bowls are only giving to the third, and the third is never giving back? The third bowl begins to overflow, making a big mess. We, too, can become lost in ourselves and our needs and wants, ruining ourselves, and starving another of their needs, if we forget to give to another. Where can you give to others with your time and talents?

Teenage Activity:
Think of a person who needs your help. Ask what you can do (listen, pray, act) Or think of where you might need some help and find a person who you believe can help you.

Adult Activity:
"Blessed to be a blessing." Are you a blessing? How? Where? To whom? Reflect upon how Jesus reached out and served his outcast neighbors. Where has God blessed you in your life? How can you share that with others?

Prayer:
Lord God, I am blessed to be called and marked as a child of God. Thank you. Help me to live a life of blessing and giving to my neighbor through . . .

Day 21

The Lord is merciful and slow to anger . . . and abounding in steadfast love.
Exodus 34:6/Psalm 145:8

Sadly, many of us grew up picturing God primarily as an angry judge. I remember reading in a high school English class, the classic sermon of the revival preacher, Jonathan Edwards, "Sinners in the Hands of an Angry God." Certainly a faithful reading of scripture sees God's "righteous" anger over idolatry, injustice and sin. That, in fact, is the context of this passage from Exodus. Moses has come down from Mount Sinai with the 10 Commandments to discover his people worshipping a golden calf. And God says "Now let me alone, so that my wrath may burn hot against them and I may consume them;" But because Moses intercedes and pleads with God, "the Lord changed his mind" (Exodus 32:14). In the giving of the 10 Commandments, God has revealed his will for his people. Now following their repentance for their sin of idolatry, God reveals his heart when he says "The Lord, the Lord, a God merciful and gracious, slow to anger and abounding in steadfast love." He goes on to say "yet by no means clearing the guilty, but visiting the iniquity of the parents upon the children and the children's children to the third and fourth generation" (Exodus 34:6-7). Once again it's is not an "either-or." God is either angry or loving. God is "both-and"; both angry over sin and merciful, slow to anger, and abounding in steadfast love. And so the Psalmist echoes this passage from Exodus and joyfully sings, "Great is the Lord, and greatly to be praised; his greatness is unsearchable" (Psalm 145:3).

Reflection Questions:
- Do you imagine God as an angry or merciful God? Why?
- How do you feel Jesus has interceded for you and showed God's love in your life?

....

....

....

....

....

....

....

....

....

....

....

The Lord is merciful and slow to anger...and abounding in steadfast love.
Exodus 34:6/ Psalm 145:8

Family Activity:

As a family, talk about the house rules. There might be many, but what are the agreed upon basics? Write the "Five Basic Family Rules" for your household. Covenant with each other to support and follow these rules. Agree that when someone breaks a rule while there may be consequences, ultimately you will be forgiving and merciful, just as God is to each of us.

Teenage Activity:

Take time to reflect on the rules you encounter in your life at school, at home, and in the world. What are 5 rules that you think God gives us to help us live healthy and happy lives? Write them in your journal (Evernote). Share with a friend!

Adult Activity:

Imagine a situation where God can help you "be slow to anger and abound and steadfast love."

Prayer:

Almighty God, abounding in steadfast love, even for me a sinner that breaks and forgets to follow rules, especially your command to love and care for all humanity and nature, forgive me, Lord. Give me your strength to be the peacemaker, the justice seeker, and the disciple of your way. May I be a living example of you in my daily living by . . .

Day 22

He that is without sin ... cast the first stone.
JOHN 8:7

The Pharisees were trying to trap Jesus when they bring to him a women caught in adultery and asked if he agreed with the Mosaic law which required the woman to be stoned. His famous answer silenced the Pharisees because they, like all people, are guilty of sin. But we humans are all too quick to judge and point the finger at other people's sins! In another incident Jesus addresses the issue of our being judgmental when he says, "remove the log from your own eye before you see the speck in your neighbor's eye" (Matthew 7:5) and "Judge not that you not be judged" (Matthew. 7:1). On one level his point is "take care of your own business." But on a more profound level he is reminding us that we all "sin and fall short of the glory of God" (Romans 3:23). We are all in need of grace and forgiveness. Earlier in John's Gospel we are told "God so loved the world that he gave his only Son, so that everyone who believes him may not perish but may have eternal life." But that's not the end of the story for John 3:16 is followed by verse 17, "Indeed, God did not send the Son into the world to condemn the world, but in order that the world might be saved through him." Because God's final word for us is mercy and forgiveness not judgment, we are called to that same life/ ministry of reconciliation. I like the way Michael Jackson says it in "The Man in the Mirror"; "I'm starting with the man in the mirror. I'm asking him to change his ways. And no message could have been any clearer. If you want to make the world a better place, take a look at yourself and then make a change."

Reflection Questions:
- What are your top three pet peeves about other people?
- When you look in the mirror, what are three things you need to change with God's help?

He that is
without sin...
cast the first
stone.
John 8:7

Family Activity:

As a family take out a piece of paper and fold it in half, length wise. On one half write "sinner" and on the same side, but below the fold mark write "saint." Take time to reflect on your actions and words toward each family member over the past week. Write a word, a phrase or create a drawing to describe you in each area. Being helpful would go under "saint." Using hurtful words would go under "sinner." After each member has had a chance to list at least one thing under each area, turn the paper over. Write bold phrases such as, Jesus is my Savior," God cares for me, etc. Hang it on the refrigerator to remind how God can turn our sins into blessings.

Teenage Activity:

Make a list of current "gossip." Tear up the list. Take sticky notes or small pieces of paper and write ways that you can be an advocate for justice and fairness in your family, school, or community. Post these in places where you will see it every morning. Start your day, committing to "be the change" by focusing on one of the items listed and doing it each day.

Adult Activity

Find a smooth stone and rinse it off. Take the stone and carry it with you for a week in your purse or pocket, place it on your desk, or in your car dashboard as a reminder of this amazing grace. And use it to remind you that Jesus did not cast the first stone, but rather cast the net of forgiveness for all.

Prayer:

Dear Lord, help us not to throw stones but to welcome and love…

Day 23

Where there is no vision . . . the people perish.
PROVERBS 29:18 (KING JAMES VERSION)

Great leaders are known for their vision. Martin Luther King, Jr. in his "I Have a Dream" speech shared his vision for a time when there would be equality, respect, justice, and love between the races. Native American chiefs go on vision quests to seek direction for their people. In Revelation, St. John shares a powerful and hopeful vision of a "new heaven and a new earth" while in prison on the island of Patmos. Visions are important for they can guide our individual lives as well. They are not just for leaders. I remember my parents telling me as a child, "You can do great things with your life." That vision has inspired me to try new things and risk failure in pursuit of my dreams. They added a Bible verse to ground my hope in God's activity in my life."I can do all things through Christ who strengthens me" (Philippians 4:13). Parents have a wonderful opportunity to paint a picture of possibility by encouraging their children to dream big and to support them in their pursuit of that dream. This little proverb has big implications for its hearers because it says that having a vision is a life-and-death issue. One of my professors said it this way, "Unless you have an idea of where you are going, you will probably end up somewhere else." We all know that our visions and dreams are often not achieved or realized, but without them our lives can be directionless and devoid of meaning. The Bible paints a vision of God's kingdom where peace, and justice, and love prevail and we are invited to join God in making that vision a reality.

Reflection Questions:
- What are your dreams?
- How is God shaping your dreams?

_____

_____

_____

_____

_____

_____

_____

_____

_____

_____

Where there is no vision... the people perish. Proverbs 29:18 (King James Version)

Family Activity:

Draw individual pictures of each family member's unique gifts/talents. Put them together to show how your family can contribute towards God's vision and kingdom on earth. Post on the door of your house.

Teenage Activity:

Write or draw what your dream/vision is for yourself and how it fits into the larger world. Hang the piece where you will see it daily.

Watch the "I have a dream" speech by Dr. Martin Luther King and imagine how you can help make that dream a reality where your world.

Adult Activity:

Write down what your dreams (1) were as a young person, (2) are now, and (3) are for the future. How have they changed or remained similar over time?

Prayer:

Dear God, you knew me before I took my first breathe of air, and when I was born you breathed life into me. Thank you for such love and hope in my life! Help me to realize that you dream for only good things for me and for your world. Help me to . . .

Day 24

Pride goes . . . before the Fall.
PROVERBS 16:18

Actually "pride goes before destruction and a haughty spirit before a fall." But aren't we supposed to take pride in our work and do our best? Certainly! But pride can easily lead to a haughty spirit and ultimately that leads to a fall. One of my mentors, Pastor Ken Olson, taught me that it all begins with the word "better." When we begin to compare ourselves with others we have two options: Suffer by comparison and feel inadequate because we don't measure up. Or, we think of ourselves and our efforts as "better." Cain felt Abel's sacrifice was better than his, so he decided to eliminate the competition and killed his brother. Perhaps our response isn't so extreme but when we play the comparison game for better or worse we all end up losers and we all fall. Whether it's nations, corporations, adults, or children we all sow the seeds of our own and other's destruction in the game of winners and losers. In the Sermon on the Mount Jesus says "Blessed are the poor in spirit" (Matthew 5:3). He teaches the disciples that the true leader is a servant and that to enter the Kingdom one must become like a little child. The prophet Micah ends his list of what God requires "Do justice, love kindness, and walk HUMBLY" (Micah 6:8). Be careful, however, that we don't turn humility into a "work" and begin to compare ourselves and become more humble than others. It is the work of the Holy Spirit, as Martin Luther taught in his explanation to the Third Article of the Apostle's Creed. "I cannot by my own reason or strength believe in my Lord Jesus, but the Holy Ghost has called me through the Gospel, enlightened me with His gifts and strengthens and preserves me in the one true faith."

Reflection Questions:

- Where has pride caused you to fall?
- What does real humility look like?

_____

_____

_____

Family Activity:

Take chalk and trace a member of the family on the driveway or sidewalk. Now draw lines of division, separating the body into the number of parts equal to the number of members of the family. Write each person's name in one area each. Now take turns sharing what that person does as a family member. Each person has a position and duties in the family. The body would not be complete without every part, without every person. Realize that no one is more important than the other, but rather all are connected and need to give support to each other for the body to work at its best ability.

Teenage Activity:

To whom do you compare yourself? List three gifts that God has given you. Write those gifts on a post-it and put them in a place to remind you how these gifts might be used in ways to help and build up yourself and the other, rather than compare and compete. Add to your screensaver with a favorite picture of yourself.

Adult Activity:

Society tells us to take pride in our works, but there is a difference between pride and arrogance. Think of a situation where your pride has turned into arrogance and caused you stumble?

Prayer:

Lord, thank you for the many gifts and talents you have entrusted in me to be used in your kingdom to give you glory. May I humbly share them to help others . . .

Day 25

I am the way, the truth, and the life . . . no one comes to the father . . .
JOHN 14:6

Like John 3:16, this passage is well known inside and outside the church. For believers, it grounds our claim that Jesus is God and in God we encounter the Father, the Creator, the first person of the Trinity. Sadly, this passage is used in a literalistic way which excludes and misses the main point of Jesus' words. When Jesus says "I am the door" and invites people to knock, seek, and find, he is not literally a door. In the same way, Jesus' description of himself as the "way, the truth, and the life" is meant to suggest to his disciples that through him they will encounter God. Does this mean that the only way to encounter God is through Jesus? No! Before Jesus' birth, God's people's knowledge and experience with God was rich and life-giving. This famous passage, called the High Priestly Prayer, is a part of Jesus' final instructions to his disciples before he left them. He comforts his followers with his promise that he is going to prepare a place for them, to intercede with the Father, and ultimately to send his Spirit, the Spirit of Truth to guide them in his absence. This beautiful word picture was not meant to say that Jesus is the only way to God, the only truth, the only life. Some will disagree with me on this point. A story might help explain my perspective. I sent out a video crew from one of my classes to ask people "What does God looks like?" Some answers were expected, like "God is like an old man." The Star Wars movies were popular at that time and a few said "God is a 'force'." (I had to laugh when one person said, "God is round!") Finally, after 40 interviews, a person said, "If you want to see what God looks like, look at Jesus!" For Christians, Jesus is the best picture we have of God. So if you want to know and experience God, look at AND follow Jesus!

Reflection Questions:

- Where have you seen or sensed God today?
- What is the easiest part of seeing God in Jesus? The hardest?

I am the way, the truth, and the life . . . no one comes to the father . . . John 14:6

Family Activity:

At dinner time or in the car ask where each has seen or encountered God in his/her day.

Teenage Activity:

Ask your friends, "Who is Jesus?" Listen thoughtfully, but don't attempt to argue or challenge what they say. Just listen. Ask yourself, "Who is Jesus for me?"

Adult Activity:

Take time at the end of the day to look back and see where God has been present in your daily activities. Share this with someone who would benefit from hearing a word of encouragement.

Prayer:

Lord Jesus and Comforter, I give praise to you for being here with me, even when I don't acknowledge your presence. Help me to see you more clearly, love you more dearly and follow you more nearly as I...

Day 26

A house divided against itself . . . cannot stand.
LUKE 11:17

This passage became famous when Abraham Lincoln used it before the Civil War to warn that the division between North and South would destroy the United States. No one doubts the "truth" in his statement, but the context in the Bible is very different. Jesus had been casting out demons and some people claimed he was "casting out demons by Beelzebub, the ruler of the demons" (Luke 11:15). To this claim Jesus utters this reply: "A house divided against its self becomes a desert, and house falls on house. If Satan also is divided against himself, how will his kingdom stand?" (Luke 11:17-18). So, what was the original point Jesus was trying to make? I think he states it clearly a few verses later "Whoever is not with me is against me and whoever does not gather with me scatters" (Luke 11:23). Lincoln was right. The passage is about unity, but Jesus calls us to be one in him. We do this individually by having the mind of Christ and corporately as members of one body his church. A home, a business, a community, a nation "divided against itself cannot stand." Lincoln understood this truth as he sought to unify a divided country. But Christians are called to a deeper loyalty and unity which Paul proclaims in Romans 6:3-4: "Do you not know that all of us who have been baptized into Christ Jesus were baptized into his death? Therefore we have been buried with him by baptism into death, so that, just as Christ was raised from the dead by the glory of the Father, so we might walk in newness of life." Our new life is united by our oneness in Christ and given an expansive and inclusive world-view, for in him there is "no longer Jew or Greek, slave or free, male or female, for all of you are one in Christ Jesus" (Galatians 3:28).

Reflection Questions:
- Where or when do you feel divided?
- Where or when do you feel united?

A house
divided
against
itself . . .
cannot stand.
Luke 11:17

....

....

....

....

....

....

....

....

Family Activity:
Each person write down one thing that is the most important thing on the family calendar. Share why. Does everyone have the same view of its importance?

Teenage Activity:
What are the things, activities, commitments, that pull you in different directions? Using symbols draw a picture depicting this. Now draw a cross through the center of your picture and ask yourself how you could be united in Christ.

Adult Activity:
Through work, school, parenting, etc., how are these commitments and responsibilities and other concerns pulling you in different directions? Try the practice of Centering Prayer and find a quiet place, close your eyes, and for 10 minutes slowly repeat the phrase "One in Christ . . ."

Prayer:
Dear Lord, you unify all your children through your son Jesus Christ and his death and resurrection. Help me to realize that I am yours through my baptism. Help me to have the mind of Christ in my interactions with . . .

Day 27

The earth is the Lord's . . . and all that is in it.
PSALM 24:1

The earth is the Lord's. This is most certainly true. God created everything and "it is good . . . very good." But why when I look out at much of creation is it not very good? The air and water are polluted, the rain forests are disappearing, deserts are spreading, species are becoming extinct, and the entire planet is threatened by gradual global warming or instantaneous nuclear annihilation. What's the problem? It began in the garden when Adam and Eve decided they knew more than the Creator. They decided that "me" was more important than "we." What was intended as a garden to feed all people and a place of enjoyment of fellow creatures and the creator became "my" property, stuff, house, car, toys, and country. When sin came to the garden, it became "my" garden. God invited us to care for (have dominion over) the garden with him, but we humans decided to use the garden for ourselves often at the expense of the garden and to the exclusion of others. So what is the solution? Like any good confirmation student knows, the answer is Jesus."For as in Adam all die, even so in Christ shall all be made alive" (1 Corinthians 15:22). Jesus is the "new Adam" who God has sent to restore our relationship with each other and the creation. The same Spirit which brooded over creation is the Holy Spirit which Christ breathes into us in our baptism and into our daily tending of our planetary garden . . . for the "Earth is the Lord's . . . and all that is in it."

Reflection Questions:
- Where are you most possessive?
- What makes it difficult for you to share?

The earth is
the Lord's . . .
and all that is
in it.
Psalm 24:1

_____

_____

_____

_____

_____

_____

_____

_____

_____

_____

Family Activity:

Fill a large bowl with water. Place an orange in the water bowl so that it can float. Now as a family, make a list of the things that you claim as your possessions. As the list grows, take the knife and slowly cut off portions the oranges' peel. Notice the more we claim as ours and not God's, the more God's world (orange) begins to suffer and sink. How can instead share our possessions with people in need both locally and around the world?

Teenage Activity:

View the journey of one your possessions (jeans) in this video: www.renters.com/video/2013/06/17/from-factory-floor-to-store-the-journey?videoId=243388736. Reflect, journal, discuss.

Adult Activity:

Make a list of all your "stuff" and mark which are "needs" and which ones are "wants." Now make a list of your absolute necessities to live.

Prayer:

Lord God Creator, thank you for the amazing gift of trust to care for this world of yours. Forgive me for not doing my best. Help me to share . . .

Day 28

If you have the faith of a mustard seed . . . you can move a mountain.
MATTHEW 17: 20-21

Well, almost. Jesus actually said, "For truly I tell you, if you have the faith of a mustard seed, you will say to this mountain, 'Move from here to there,' and it will move; and nothing will be impossible for you." What is the most powerful force on the planet? Is it nuclear energy? How about laser technology? Is it the power of the sun? No, it's faith. That's what Jesus is saying. What is faith? It's more than believing in a bunch of things. Faith is the active belief that what we imagine or dream can actually happen. Notice I said active belief. We first need to believe but equally important is taking steps to put our faith into action. Otherwise you are just a dreamer. Okay, okay, it says "move mountains." Can we move mountains? Certainly not by just sitting and concentrating our mental energy on a pile of rocks! But harness your idea and put it into action (hard work) and "shazzam" dynamite has been invented and then "zipp-zapp" a bull-dozer moves the rubble. You get my point. But is that what Jesus is getting at . . . maybe a little bit. I think he is talking about something even more amazing . . . moving the mountains in the landscape of the human heart. Jesus' disciples had tried unsuccessfully to cast out demons. Jesus says they lack faith. He is teaching them that it takes more than just saying the right words or reciting a formula to really change things. Will faith always literally move a mountain? No! But faith in action empowered by God's spirit can be the most powerful force for good on the planet. Try it!

Reflection Questions:
- What are the "mountains" in your life?
- Where have you seen "mountains" moved by active faith?

_____

_____

_____

_____

_____

_____

_____

_____

_____

_____

_____

_____

_____

_____

_____

_____

_____

_____

If you have the faith of a mustard seed...you can move a mountain. Matthew 17: 20-21

Family Activity:

Identify a time when you accomplished something that you thought was impossible (individually/group). What role did faith play? What is something impossible or a mountain your family could move with faith?

Teenage Activity:

What is a mountain you would like to move with God's help? What are 3 steps you need to take? Write them in your journal (or Evernote).

Adult Activity:

Identify a big challenge or mountain in your neighborhood or at work and gather folks together and explore ways to be the "moving crew."

Prayer:

Help us to move with your help the mountains and walls in our lives that we create . . .

Day 29

Honor your father and your mother . . . so that your days may be long and that it may go well with you.
DEUTERONOMY 5:16

To some folks this passage sounds old-fashioned and out-of-touch with the times. To others it may be painful, because of abuse or neglect. What are we to make of the Ten Commandments today? For many they are the "Ten Suggestions" or simply irrelevant. But in God's design this wisdom is more important than ever. A stable and loving family/ household is essential to healthy and successful young people. Both experience and an enormous amount of research suggest this is true. So why honor parents? The answer is right there: "so that your days may be long and that it may go well with you." Only three of the Ten Commandments add a reason for obeying them. In ancient times there was no safety net like Social Security, pensions, or health insurance to care for older people. It was the responsibility of children to ultimately care for their parents . . . as part of honoring them. In very utilitarian terms, if you honor and care for your parents in their old age they will live longer and well. By logical extension when you are older, your children will honor and care for you. So it was a good system long ago, but what about today? Have you noticed what has happened to pensions and Social Security? At best such "retirement" programs are meant to be a supplement and at worst they may not be around when our kids grow old. Maybe it's time to dust off the third commandment and once again honor our parents. Certainly a safety net is needed to care for children and adults who fall through the cracks. But can you think of a better foundation for healthy communities and world than a family with loving parents who are honored by their children?

Reflection Questions:
- How have you honored your parents or other older adults in your community?
- How can you parent/mentor someone outside your family?

Family Activity:
Around the family table ask, how do we "honor" each other? How do children honor parents or grandparents. As a household how do we honor elderly neighbors or friends? Add to your prayers the names of those you wish to honor.

Teenage Activity:
List all the responsibilities you see your parents/caregivers take on. How do you or can you help and contribute to your household? Set your smart phone to remind you of how you can help.

Adult Activity:
What does "honoring" mean for adults honoring their parents or others who have cared for you in your life? How are you an example to your children and grandchildren on honoring?

Prayer:
Dear Heavenly Father, you have given me the very breath of life and I am so grateful. Help me to give care and honor to those that have also been my earthly parents. Provide me the time and energy and compassion to . . .

Day 30

To whom much is given . . . much will be required.
Luke 12:48

I think it was my second grade teacher who first wrote on my report card, "He has a lot of potential, but . . ." Variations on that theme followed me through my early school years until something clicked and I began to do what another teacher suggested "Apply yourself." Jesus has just told a parable about the wise and foolish servant/slaves. We all know the story about the wise servant who multiplied the master's assets and the foolish servant who buried the assets. The punch-line or moral of the story is "To whom much is given . . ." Does that phrase sound like a threat? On one level it is a warning to not waste our gifts, talents, and abilities. And perhaps, like me, we need to hear that kind of reminder. But when I look back at those who warned me, the phrase came more as a promise. My teachers, parents and coaches saw gifts in me that I wasn't using. Their words came as encouragement to be "all that I could be" and were delivered with love and grace. Well, most of the time. We live in a society which is constantly measuring our performance. Like the foolish servant in the story, we may out of fear bury our talents. Another phrase I often heard as a boy was "we are blessed to be a blessing." The message was clear that my blessings were to be shared with others, not hoarded. What would happen if we as a nation took these words to heart and out of our abundance shared generously with the rest of the world and became the #1 food sharer in the world rather than the #1 weapons seller? Jesus parable about the Final Judgement is very clear about feeding the hungry, clothing the naked, healing the broken, visiting the prisoner. There ultimately will be a "final" . . . much will be required. Remember how blessed we are and out of thankful hearts use, celebrate and share God's abundant gifts!

Reflection Questions:

- What are your unique gifts and talents? What have others told you about your abilities?
- What is your abundance? How can you share it?

To whom
much is
given...
much will
be required.
Luke 12:48

Family Activity:

Many American homes are filled with lots of things. Using the motto, "If you haven't used it in a year, you probably don't need it." Have each member go throughout the house and find five items (or more!) they feel are abundant in the house. Discuss as a family who might benefit from these things and then go and give!

Teenage Activity:

Make a list of 10 items (include technology) that you see in your room that you feel are abundant and that you don't need. (There is a difference between needs and wants.) After you have made a list, now think about who you know could use these items. They could be people you personally know, or a community organization. After your list is complete with items and future owners, go give these items away.

Adult Activity:

Make a list of 10 things (talents, time, things) that God has gifted you in abundance and share 3 with someone who needs them. Consider how you might allocate (tithe) from your material wealth for the good of others and the world.

Prayer:

God you have gifted me with so much, including time, talents and possessions. With these gifts I will . . .

Day 31

This is the day the Lord has made . . . let us rejoice and be glad in it.
PSALM 118:24

Are you a morning person? If not, this passage may sound annoying at best and impossible at worst. My dad was a morning person. He usually popped out of bed with a smile on his face and often with a song on his lips. In fact, when he died and was eulogized he was described as happy, cheerful, friendly, and welcoming. While much can be learned about temperament and perhaps each of us has a default disposition as morning/evening persons, this psalm proclaims boldly "This is the day the Lord has made, let us rejoice and be glad in it." It grounds our joy and gladness not in how I am feeling, but in God's provision of a new day. We aren't to ignore our pain, frustrations and struggles. There are plenty of Psalms which are brutally honest in their sharing the darkness in life.

I had a paper route when I was a kid. A crusty old guy named Gordon delivered my bundle of Des Moines Register's each Sunday to the drop-off spot. As he puffed on his cigar he would grumble each week, "Well, I didn't find my name in the obituaries, so I guess God ain't ready for me yet." Gordon was on the right track. I hated alarm clocks in high school.

One summer at church camp our counselor woke us each morning with a song I have never forgotten, "This is the day. . ." I couldn't get the song out of my mind each day. And annoying as it was, the message has stayed with me. Yes, the Bible teaches that life is "a veil of tears" (Psalm 84:6). But the Psalmist doesn't let us off the hook to dwell in a perpetual pity-party when he sings "This is the day . . ." In the midst of our worst days may these words echo in our minds, and hearts, and lives!

Reflection Questions:

- Where have you seen God in the course of the day?
- How do you celebrate the day and life that God has given to you?

This is the day the Lord has made...let us rejoice and be glad in it. Psalm 118:24

Family Activity:

Create a centerpiece on the family table which includes three items from each person for which they are thankful. At meals invite people to explain the item and weave your thanks and into your rejoicing and glad prayers .

Teenage Activity:

Read Psalm 118 and then write in your journal (Evernote) a Psalm which shares your thoughts and feelings. Share with a friend and God!

Adult Activity:

As you begin your day take several deep breaths and give thanks to God for the gift of life and breath. Count your blessings! Enter into the day's activities with spirit of gratitude and with an eye for seeing God at work in big and small ways.

Prayer:

Lord, you who made the sun and stars and moon. I am thankful for a new day. Open my eyes to see . . .

Day 32

God's foolishness . . . is wiser than human wisdom.
1 CORINTHIANS 1:25

The cost of a college education is skyrocketing, often top-
ping $50,000 a year. Is it worth it? Good question. Perhaps a
degree once was a ticket to a job, but not anymore. What's
the point? I think we all agree on the value of a good education because it expands our knowledge and prepares us
to be responsible citizens. But, does a good education lead
to wisdom? The Apostle Paul said, "Where is the one who is
wise? Where is the scribe? Where is the debater of this age?
Has not God made foolish the wisdom of the world . . . For
Jews demand signs and Greeks demand wisdom, but we pro-
claim Christ crucified, a stumbling block to Jews and foolishness to Gentiles, but to those who are called, both Jews and
Greeks, Christ the power of God and the wisdom of God" (1
Corinthians 1:20-24). Are you a "Jew" who needs God to demonstrate his power through a "sign?" Or, are you a "Greek" who
is looking for "wisdom" through a rational answer? Better look
somewhere else for God, for God's wisdom is the foolishness
of Christ dying on the cross, his power is manifest in being the
servant of all. God's wisdom is found in the paradox of dying
to find life, serving to lead, giving to receive, emptying to be
filled. We live in the midst of a knowledge explosion, but the
world's problems continue to multiply. God's wisdom calls us
to be fools for Christ who "love our enemies, pray for those
who mistreat us, bless those who curse us, forgive those who
have wronged us" (Matthew 5:44). It may not lead to a job or
a degree, but here's the promise: "Give, and it will be given to
you. A good measure, pressed down, shaken together, running over, will be put in your lap; for the measure you give will
be the measure you get back" (Luke 6:38).

Reflection Questions:

- What is one of the greatest pieces of wisdom you have ever received?
- What does it mean to you to be "fools for Christ?"

God's foolishness... is wiser than human wisdom.
1 Corinthians 1:25

Family Activity:

Think about an apple. An apple provides a great snack and good nutrition. However, for more apple trees to be planted to grow more apples, one must get the seeds from an existing apple. Death must come to the existing apple to help grow another tree. Read Shel Silverstein's *The Giving Tree*, and talk about how each family member can give to receive.

Teenage Activity:

View this clip from *Pay It Forward*, then journal, and finally share with a friend. www.youtube.com/watch?v=5ZTm-iYUpm4

Adult Activity:

Often those who have very little (the poor and people in the developing world) show amazing generosity and joy in feeding and caring for visitors to their homes. How can I learn from the "least of these" and share God's foolish and extravagant love in my daily life?

Prayer:

Lord, thank you for your foolishness in forgiving and in loving me. Help me to be a "fool for Christ's sake" by . . .

Day 33

Father, forgive them . . . for they don't know what they are doing.
Luke 23:34

Remember when you got in a fight with your sister or brother, and your parents made you shake hands or hug and say "I'm sorry"? I hated that drill. It was a drill, wasn't it? It was "practice" then and it needs to be repeated over and over again in our lives, because forgiveness is the hardest thing to do. As much as we like to think of ourselves as caring, altruistic, forgiving people, our instinctive response (original sin) is to get back at someone. Perhaps the only difference between childhood vengeance and that of adults is we adults cover our tracks better. Whether it leads to violence as it did when Cain killed his brother Abel or simply a hateful thought, our human response is often not far removed from our primate ancestors. The 6th Commandment, "Thou shalt not kill," was a major step forward from blood vengeance which was common among ancient civilizations. Jesus took it a huge step further in his Sermon on the Mount when he equates hateful thoughts with murder. And ultimately he practices what he preaches from the cross when he prays, "Father forgive them . . ." as a prayer for those who were crucifying him. Forgiveness is the hardest and the best thing we can do. Don Henley sings "It's the heart of the matter." Forgiveness starts with confessing and admitting our own wronging of others. And then we experience the best thing: as we forgive someone and wipe the slate clean, we simultaneously erase and let go of the anger, pain, burden bringing reconciliation and peace between people.

Reflection Questions:
- What is the hardest thing or person you've forgiven?
- What is one thing you need forgiveness for now? From whom?

_____

_____

_____

_____

_____

_____

_____

_____

_____

_____

Father,
forgive
them . . .
for they
don't know
what they
are doing.
Luke 23:34

Family Activity:

As a family, set aside time once a week where everyone will be home. Sit around the table or some place to be comfortable. Hand out note cards, two per person. One is for offering forgiveness, and one is for asking for forgiveness. Write "Forgive me" on one and "I forgive you" on the other. If there are family members that cannot write, do this part for them. (small children can draw symbols of each) As each is able and ready, hand the card to the person you need to give it to. Talk, share, listen, love and forgive. Make this a regular activity in the family.

Teenage Activity:

Use the following Forgiveness Guidelines in one specific situation in your life: 1. Recognize the need, 2. Pray for God's spirit, 3. Invite the counsel of a wise friend, 4. Pray again, 5. Ask for or Invite forgiveness.

Adult Activity:

From whom do you need to ask forgiveness? Don't let pride hold you back from this much needed act. Forgiving does not mean forgetting, but saying "I am sorry" can be the first step toward reconciliation. How about a card, flowers, chocolates?

Prayer:

Lord, forgive me, for I know not what I do. I am grateful for your unconditional love and forgiveness through your son Jesus Christ. Help me to live this grace of forgiveness through…

Day 34

He who lives by the sword . . . will die by the sword.
MATTHEW 26:52

There is a lot packed into this little phrase. Jesus isn't just saying he doesn't want Peter to use violence to defend him in the garden. He is also saying his kingdom doesn't use violence as a tool. Many faithful Jews thought the long-awaited Messiah would liberate Israel from the Romans and that wouldn't come without spilling blood. The reign of God Jesus was inaugurating wouldn't be based on the power of the military but on the non-violent power of love. Have we really taken to heart Jesus' words? What about the Crusades in the Middle Ages? The churches blessing of colonial conquest in the Americas? The silence of people of faith in the face of domestic violence, human trafficking, and wars across the planet? Today we may not "pick up a sword" like Peter, but doesn't our inaction in the face of violence makes us accessories? Not long after Peter put his sword away, he and the disciples deserted him and fled. Here we see the normal human pattern of fight or flight in the face of a threat. Jesus offers a third-way of non-violent resistance and love. There was blood shed but it was Jesus' own blood on the cross. We are called to take up our cross and follow him. In the face of violence, we are commanded to turn the other cheek. We are taught to go the extra mile when asked to help. We are to learn to love our enemies. This force for good was unleashed when Jesus rose from the dead and sent his followers then and now to "Go and make disciples of all nations baptizing them in the name of the Father, Son, and Holy Spirit, and teaching them to obey everything that I have commanded you. And remember, I am with you always, to the end of the age" (Matthew 28: 19-20).

Reflection Questions:

- Who is an enemy you need to love?
- Where have you caused harm or been an "accessory" to it?

He who lives by the sword... will die by the sword. Matthew 26:52

_____

_____

_____

_____

_____

Family Activity:

Draw and cut out a large cross. In the middle write down areas where you need to "turn the other cheek." Put the cross on the mirror and practice saying "I turn the other cheek when . . ." Have each family member share an example.

Peacemaking Tips: 1. Be Safe: If in danger of physical harm, call for help (parent, teacher, police) and/or leave the situation, 2. If Safe: Listen carefully, imagine and share peacemaking ideas/ options, 3. Pray for a peaceful spirit for yourself and others.

Teenage Activity:

Draw three swords and cut them out to put back together in the shape of a cross. Remember that Christ did not use the sword, but instead told others to put down their swords. Draw or write those things that cause you to want to use violent words/action rather than love to bring about peace. Make the cross your tool, not the sword.

Adult Activity:

Where have you seen violence, pain or suffering, and turned away rather than acted to bring comfort or peace? Where can your voice be of use? Write or call your local politician about a justice issue dear to you, and ask for action. Get involved.

Prayer:

Lord, make me an instrument of your peace. Guide me to . . .

Day 35

The love of money . . . is the root of all evil.
1 TIMOTHY 6:10

This famous passage is one of the most misquoted in the Bible as people often say "money is the root of all evil." It's the "love of" money that's the problem. Money is simply a tool for placing a value on the exchange of goods and services. Ever hear the phrase "money is power?" It's true, isn't it? Who has the most stuff? Who wins elections? Who gets what they want? Humans are acquisitive creatures. We like to acquire things. Some are necessities, some are luxuries, and money gives us the power to surround ourselves with what we need and what we want. Wisdom is in knowing the difference between the two. Wisdom is knowing when we have enough. One of my teachers put his finger on the real issue when he said, "Don't let your possessions 'possess' you." When our stuff comes before God and our neighbor, then we are in trouble. But it's hard, isn't it? You buy a new car and it's easy to focus an enormous amount of time and energy around caring for it and thinking about it. Anything can become an idol- even good things. Ever notice how hard it is to go through your closet and decide what to give away? Your library? Your garage? Perhaps the most insidious danger of the "love of $" is when we use it to evaluate ourselves or others. It's easy to look up to the rich and look down upon the poor. Remember in her "magnificat" that Mary rejoices because God "sends away the rich empty handed and exalts the humble" (Luke 1:53). Throughout scripture and embodied in Jesus, God's care for the poor is emphasized over and over. But whether we are rich or poor or middle class, each of us is made in God's image and is loved as we are not because of what we have. That's good news!

Reflection Questions:
- How do you "love" money?
- What is an idol in your life?

Family Activity:
Create a family "bank" and begin putting your spare change in it each day. At the end of the year use the $ to purchase a gift from Heiffer International (rabbit, cow, bees, ducks etc) for a family.

Or create a bank which has three sections (or order from Thrivent). For others, for college, and for fun. Practice putting equal amounts in each section. Each year donate the amount collected "for others" to a worthy organization (church, BFW, Habitat, Heiffer Project).

Teenage Activity:
Write down where you spend your time in a day. How many hours sleeping, eating, school, work, homework, friends, family, music, video games, computer time? What truly are your needs versus your wants. Where are your priorities aligned with God values? (Download the Spendee app which will help you track your use of money...)

Adult Activity:
What needs do you have? What needs have you witnessed others longing for? How can you fulfill the needs of others out of your excess? Consider the biblical mandate to give 10% (tithe) to your church/charities.

Prayer:
Lord, you are the Alpha and the Omega and the focus of all that is living. Help me to realize the idols that I place before you and to not have my life ruled by their possession. Lead me to . . .

Day 36

Go into the world ... and make disciples of all nations.
MATTHEW 28:18-20

Imagine the conversation between the disciples: What did Jesus say? I heard, "Go!" I remember something about "make disciples." What about his words, "into all the world … to all nations?" What do you hear in Jesus' words today? I first hear that we are to stop standing around and get busy. We are to "Go into all the world . . . to all nations." The message Jesus proclaimed and lived isn't meant to be kept in a small number of chosen people. When I was a boy, our church sent a missionary to Japan to share this message. I contributed my pennies and every few years she would come and share stories of her experiences at our congregation. For a long time that was my understanding of the Great Commission: send someone, but not me. A friend has written a book describing this faulty thinking as the Great Omission. Part of my resistance came from the phrase "make disciples." In college this sounded like a mechanistic process of creating cookies with a cookie cutter. But wasn't Jesus' encounter with each of his disciples different? Each was called to follow but his approach to a fisherman, tax collector, a leper, or a prostitute was different. And so it is with us today. Each of us has a faith story which tells how God has been active in our lives. It may have been through many small acts of love in a caring and faith-filled family. It may have occurred in a dramatic conversion experience. Whatever the story Jesus tells us to do two things: Go into our world near or far and share our story. And, equally important, invite those we encounter at school, work, or play to share their story.

Reflection Questions:
- What is your faith story?
- With whom have you shared it lately?

....

....

....

....

....

....

....

....

....

....

....

....

....

....

....

....

Go into the world... and make disciples of all nations. Matthew 28:18-20

Family Activity:

Make a list of all the people you interact with everyday. Who have you spoken to about your love of God? Make a commitment to speak up, and share your love of Christ with at least one person on your list.

Teenage Activity:

Make a list of all your friends. Make a list of all the people you want to get to know. Who have you taken lately to a church activity? Any? Commit to share this part of your life with one person from your list.

Adult Activity:

When was the last time you shared your faith story with your family? A friend? Maybe it's easier to write than speak it. Either way, share your faith story and your love of God with another person this week and invite them to share their story.

Prayer:

Lord Jesus, you have gifted each of us with a unique story. Thank you. Help me to have the strength and passion to . . .

Day 37

The one who believes and is baptized . . . you will be saved.
MARK 16:16

Believe, baptize, saved. Three words filled with meaning. They are also often interpreted differently and become the cause of disagreement and division. What would Jesus say today? I think his response would be simple and clear. Jesus: "When I say believe, I am saying trust me. Trust me, my teaching, my words and my actions and follow me. My way is not the way of the world which focuses on me but on loving God and your neighbor. My death on a cross shows how my way of self-sacrifice threatens the way the world operates. When you 'take up your cross and follow me' you are choosing to die to yourself and live for others. In dying you will find life and life abundantly." Baptize: "Stop fighting over how you baptize and when you baptize. Whether you sprinkle or dunk infants or older folks, baptism is receiving a gift from me of new life. It's not something I do. The water washes away our sin. In the water we die to ourselves and rise to a new way of living. I like Martin Luther's reminder that we remember our baptism each day as we arise and wash and bathe. We never stop needing to bathe and be reminded of my gift of forgiveness and love." Saved: "Stop going around trying to figure out who is saved and who isn't saved. As you live your life as a believing and baptized follower invite others into that journey with you. Tell your story. Your story involves being saved from something and being saved for someone The literal meaning of the Latin word, salve, (from which we get "saved") is "wholeness." It's like the Hebrew word, shalom. So, being saved ultimately means being all that you were created to be and offering your life to God and others for the salvation of the world.

Reflection Questions:

- How do you celebrate your baptism?
- How do you share the gift of salvation with others?

The one who believes and is baptized . . . you will be saved.
Mark 16:16

Family Activity:

Go for a walk by a stream or a lake (of bowl of water on table) and wade in the water. Tell the story of Jesus' baptism. Tell the story of your baptism and how your faith has grown in your life. Invite all to "remember their baptism" and how baptism brought you into God's family.

Teenage Activity:

Ask your parents about your baptism story. What happened? Who was there? Write a new chapter of your story focusing on how you can be a tool in God's world to support others in their faith journey.

Adult Activity:

Next time you are in the shower or tub, trace the letters "baptized" on the wall and remember that you are saved by God's grace for the restoration and healing of the world. Share your story with a friend and invite them to church.

Prayer:

Lord, I thank you for your gift of baptism! Help me to . . .

Day 38

Just for fun #1: "Whatever"

If you spend any time with teenagers, you have heard this phrase. It is often accompanied by a disdainful rolling of the eyes and the end of discussion. You might think this phrase certainly isn't in the bible . . . But it is! Let me tell you a story. We were at Holden Village, a retreat center high in the Cascade Mountains planning the annual May Youth Weekends. It had been a long day and folks were ready to relax. We were struggling to find a theme for the program, when finally one of the young people said "Whatever!" She had had enough and really didn't have the energy to keep discussing. Then one of the other kids shouted "Whatever?! Isn't that in the Bible?" A quick search found the wonderful passage from Philippians 4:8-9: "Whatever is true, whatever is honorable, whatever is just, whatever is pure, whatever is pleasing, whatever is commendable, if there is any excellence and if there is anything worthy of praise, think about these things. Keep on doing the things that you have learned and received and heard and seen in me, and the God of peace will be with you." A "whatever" meant to end discussion started a new conversation and provided a very rich theme for our program. On the front of our sweatshirts was simply "Whatever...." On the back was the chapter and verse in the bible. You can't imagine how many "second-looks" and conversations this "whatever" started. Sometimes just an ordinary, everyday word can take on extraordinary meaning when seen with biblical eyes. Spiritual writer and friend, Mark Yaconelli, suggests that "whatever" is a wonderful one-word prayer to begin the day. Can you think of a better way to communicate our faith in God's presence and our openness to His leading than that one word?

Reflection Questions:

Just for fun #1: "Whatever"

- What is one word that brings you closer to God in your day?
- Where is it and how is it used in the Bible?

Family Activity:

What word(s) do you hear used a lot lately? What meaning does it carry for you? Did this word or phrase exist in Jesus time? Brainstorm what meanings this word could have had in Jesus' time and how he would have responded.

Teenage Activity:

Is there a word or phrase you hear a lot from adults around you? Maybe it's "when you're older, you'll understand" or "when I was your age." What wisdom might there be in their words?

Adult Activity:

Are there acronyms you see in young people's texts or Facebook posts that confuse you? "BTW" or "JK," for example. Write them down and ask a younger person what these mean.

Prayer:

Lord, we thank you for your words of grace and guidance. Help me to understand the importance of words and to use them more wisely. Let me be more open to . . .

Day 39

Just for fun #2: "Oh, well . . ."

When friend and author Mark Yaconelli suggested "whatever" as a great one-word prayer to begin my day, he also had an excellent idea for a simple two-word prayer to end my day: "Oh, well." Once again we have a common phrase I hear from my kids at home and in the classroom. Generally they roll their eyes with this one, too. They imply they have nothing to say or to contribute because the decision has already been made. It's a *fait accompli*, so "Oh, well," why fight it? But looking through biblical eyes "whatever" can convey something far deeper. While "whatever" can signal our trust and openness to God in the day to come, "Oh, well" can be recognition that what has occurred during the day has been in God's hands. I think of the wonderful hymn: "When peace like a river attends my way, When sorrows like sea billows roll. Whatever my lot, you have taught me to say, It is well, it is well with my soul." I am a list-maker. At the end of my day I look to see how many of the tasks I have checked off. Too often I evaluate my day by how much I have accomplished. There is certainly a value in setting goals and in working to accomplish them, but sometimes this organizational tool seeps into my own sense of self-worth and I feel like a failure or at least that the value of the day was low. Praying "Oh, well…" helps me remember that God uses and blesses my large and small efforts. Laying my head on the pillow offering an "Oh, well" allows me to offer my day and my life to God and to rest in God's care. And that is rest for body and soul!

Reflection Questions:
- How do you measure a good day?
- What prayer do you use at the end of each day?

Family Activity:

Trace a person's hand on paper. At the end of each day write "God's hands" in the traced outline. Post this where everyone can add their words to God for the day.

Teenage Activity:

Make a list of your major stressors each day (at least 5). As you end the day circle two stressors and give them to God by crossing them off your list.

Adult Activity:

Close your day with an ancient prayer practice called the Examen by asking where did you see God's activity and where was God absent. End your prayer with thanks to God and "oh, well!"

Prayer:

Lord, I start my day with trust in you, in the "whatever" moments that will be. Thank you for being with me always. I end my day giving praise and thanks and handing over all my worries to you Lord, in the words of . . .

Day 40

Just for Fun #3: "And they lived happily ever after"

It all started with "in the beginning." How does the story end? "And they lived happily ever after" of course! Isn't that the way all of the fairy tales end? The prince comes along and with a kiss brings Sleeping Beauty back to life. When the shoe fits Cinderella is on her way to becoming a queen. Mircea Eliade, in his book Myth and Reality, points out that many folk tales wrestle with the issues of evil and good, life and death. The Brothers Grimm collected many of these stories and the original tales are often much darker than Disney's animated versions. Most of our kids know these simpler cartoon versions and can sing along to the catchy music. So, what's the problem? If we take a look around we have to admit that much of life is not pleasant, easy, or happy. In our attempt to keep our kids safe we overly sanitize the problems in life and shelter them from life's harsh realities. In a sense we live in a fairy tale world and ignore the details of the story and hope that our story will end "and they lived happily ever after." That's why the Bible and its stories are so important. When we read it we find all the issues of fallible human beings: lust, corruption, murder, and jealousy. We also find a solution to those problems that leads to the gruesome death of God's son, Jesus. But, like Disney, we often quickly move past Good Friday to the resurrection on Easter as our "and they lived happily ever after." When Jesus says "Take up your cross and follow me" he is inviting us into a new way of living which doesn't ignore or deny the painful issues of life. Instead, led by God's spirit we enter into those realities and die to ourselves so that we find new life, real life, resurrected life, in Jesus Christ. And both now and at the end of our lives we experience abundant and eternal life . . . happily ever after . . . yes . . . but far more!

Reflection Questions:

Just for Fun #3: "And they lived happily ever after."

- How has your life demonstrated (or not) the "happily ever after?"
- How does the reality of Good Friday make you feel?

_____

_____

_____

_____

_____

_____

_____

_____

_____

_____

Family Activity:

Share your "highs, lows" and "Yay God" around a circle. By sharing our low and high points of the day, we can focus on the gratitude we have for God in our lives.

Teenage Activity:

What fairy tale do you believe in? Why? How does the story of Jesus change your view of "happily ever after"?

Adult Activity:

What painful story have you heard or seen on the news lately? Take a newspaper and mark a cross on the articles that show the self destruction of humanity. How can you take up your cross in one specific situation this week?

Prayer:

Lord Jesus, may your story be told through me. May my sins be forgiven and made happily ever after in you. Help me to…

Day 41

Just for fun #4: "Did Adam eat the apple?"

This is a question I ask my students. How would you answer the question? What does the Bible say? Let's see, the serpent tempted Eve and she persuaded Adam to eat the apple. Yes, Adam ate the apple. Sound like a trick question? Did they both eat an apple? Did he just take a bite? Eventually someone asks, "Was it an apple?" You are getting warmer! The bible says that they both "ate" and the "fruit" came from the "tree that is in the middle of the garden." So, in truth, we don't know what kind of fruit they ate. So what kind of fruit was it? It certainly could have been an apple. Apple cultivars originated in the Middle East over 4,000 years ago. Some scholars believe it may have been the more common pomegranate. We do know that "it was good for food and a delight to the eyes." Ultimately, the kind of fruit our ancestors in the faith ate isn't important. What is important is that they believed that eating the fruit would make them wise. This is certainly a noble goal, but what the serpent actually said to Eve was "You will not die; for God knows that when you eat of it your eyes will be opened and you will be like God, knowing good and evil" (Genesis 3:4-8). In eating of the fruit, they crossed the line between being creature and creator. Like Adam and Eve, we want to be in control. Rather than keeping God at the center of the Garden of life, we place ourselves, at the center of our lives, with God as a hedge at the periphery. When we look in the mirror we have to confess our nakedness before a God who simply asks to us to keep him at the center. In Jesus, the new Adam, God covers our nakedness with his righteousness and restores our relationship. And so we come to the table to be fed with bread and wine, for "the forgiveness of sins" and we are sent out to work with God to share the bounty of his garden.

Reflection Questions:
- What does the apple represent in your life?
- What do you wish to have complete control over or knowledge of? Why?

Just for fun #4: "Did Adam eat the apple?"

Family Activity:
Place an apple in the middle of the table and say there will be contest to grab the apple. Play the game several times in such a way that you win and get the apple. Change the rules. After complaints from the "losers" explain the connection with the tree in the Garden of Eden and how we humans think we are fair, but often cheat. God wants us to be fair and to share. End by cutting up the apple and sharing!

Teenage Activity:
Think of a situation where you let go of your need to be "in control' and let God be in charge and how that worked out "for good." Journal/share.

Adult Activity:
What is an area of your life where you feel God has taught you and that wisdom has made a big difference ?

Prayer:
Lord, thank you for restoring me to you through your son Jesus. Help me to let go of my cravings for . . .

Day 42

Just for fun #5 . . . three wise men?

How many wise men were there who came to visit the newborn Jesus? Three? Why? Three kids dressed up as wise men in the Christmas pageant? The Christmas hymn, "We three Kings of Orient are bearing gifts we traveled afar." Three gifts: gold, frankincense, and myrrh. Is three kings your final answer? The bible simply says, "wise men from the East came to Jerusalem" (Matthew 2:1). We really don't know how many wise men there were, but the tradition has grown to tell us there were three. How do such traditions develop? Stories are told, songs are sung, rituals are repeated, and over time a tradition develops. I often chide young students who criticize "older" people for being so traditional by reminding them that often when an activity is repeated a couple times, it becomes a tradition for them, too. In Fiddler on the Roof, Tevye talks about how traditions give order and balance to our lives, which can keep us from falling "off the roof." Some have great value and others are simply habits. We humans are habitual creatures who sometimes choose, but rather often fall into, patterns of behavior. Ever notice how we tend to sit in the same pew in church or the same seat in class? The Latin verb *traditere* means to "deliver or hand over or entrust." Thus, a tradition has a way of delivering or handing over wisdom between people from one time to another. In this way a tradition can provide a sense of comfort, knowledge, and security. But a tradition can also become a rut when it keeps us from being open to new insights and possibilities. Jesus talked about this when he warned that we not put "new wine in old wineskins" (Mark 2:22). Knowing the actual number of wise men probably doesn't make a lot of difference in our lives, but it could prompt us to ask "why do we do what we do?" How many wise men are there today?

Reflection Questions:
- What is a favorite tradition your family practices?
- What is a tradition you don't care for? Why?

Just for fun #5
Three wise
men?

Family Activity:
Think of a family tradition (seasonal, vacations, special foods) and find out who started it and why. What have you learned from that tradition? How does it shape your identity as a family?

Teenage Activity:
What is a tradition you would like to continue or create when you have your own family? Why?

Adult Activity:
What new tradition has started in your family with children and grandchildren that you value? Think of old tradition which has grown stale that you could breath new life into.

Prayer:
Lord may you be the constant tradition in my life that never grows old and pointless. Help me to better understand . . .

Day 43

Not in the Bible #1: Moderation in all things. (Aristotle)

I am not sure when I first heard this phrase, but it probably came in response to one extreme form of behavior or
another that I was guilty of. That's part of my personality. I
am not cautious; I go "all in." If a line was drawn in the sand
which I should not cross, I took it as a personal challenge to
stick my big toe over the line."Push the limits" could be my
middle name. Maybe that's why I found distance running to
so attractive."You can't run a marathon!" was all I needed to
hear to begin training for and completing this long and painful 26.2 mile race. Then I heard about the Iron Man Triathlon
and the Western States Endurance Run (100 miles). Two more
extreme sports limits that I added to my trophy shelf. If only I
had listened to "moderation in all things" I probably wouldn't
have sore knees which required replacement surgery. This
sage advice from Aristotle, not the Bible, if heeded, would, no
doubt, lead to less "-isms" with alcohol, drugs, work, and other
forms of excessive behavior. But how does this golden mean
stack up against a biblical faith? Do we want a moderate faith?
In the Parable of the Sower, the farmer throws seeds all over
the place. The Good Shepherd is willing to leave the flock for
the one lost sheep. The love we are to have for others begins with "dying to ourselves." Jesus calls us to "take up our
cross and follow." We are even called to "love your enemies."
Pretty extreme behavior? God's very nature to love excessively
is most fully expressed in the life, death, and resurrection of
Jesus. Moderation has its place, but the God's love teaches us
that "going the extra mile" is what it is all about.

Reflection Questions:
- What are some of your excessive behaviors where mod-
  eration might be wise?
- Where might you practice a more excessive or risky faith?

Not in the
Bible #1:
Moderation
in all things.
(Aristotle)

Family Activity:

Have you ever eaten so much you felt sick? Some excessive-ness causes us pain. But God's excessiveness is good for our sake! Prepare several loaves of home-made bread and slowly eat, and savor, and discuss how much is "enough." Give thanks and share the extra bread with your neighbors!

Teenage Activity:

Create a continuum with Passive on one extreme and Excessive on the other. Where are you on that continuum faith-wise? Where do you want to be?

Adult Activity:

Where might God be calling you to be more bold in your love for neighbor and world?

Prayer:

Lord, I confess that my excessiveness is not always in you. Help me to find balance, and to practice . . .

Day 44

Not in Bible #2: This too shall pass.
(Sufi/Persian wisdom from the Middle Ages)

Things are going badly. A relationship has ended. Your teen-age son is being obnoxious. Your finances are in disarray. "This too shall pass." Can you hear it? Yes, things will get better. It's another phrase which has been passed down and become part of the accepted wisdom we share in difficult times. Its origin, however, is not the Bible, but Sufi wisdom from Persia. While not biblical it certainly does reflect elements of biblical wisdom. The writer of Ecclesiastes reminds us "To everything there is a season, a time to be born, a time to die, a time to plant, a time to reap" (Ecclesiastes 3:2). Whatever season of the year or our lives we find ourselves in, there is another season coming. When we think life can't get worse, we would be wise to remember that change is coming. Perhaps the only con-stant in life is change. The writer of the Psalms often laments present difficulties and then counsels that those who "wait upon the Lord" will be delivered (Isaiah 40:31). But here our attitude shouldn't be passive waiting, but active reliance on God to vindicate his people whose lives manifest justice, righ-teousness, and holiness. The prophets also pick up this theme with their warnings against idolatry and their call to "do justice, love kindness, and walk humbly" (Micah 6:8). The current situ-ation will pass as God's people actively are part of the solution. Things will change. We can be sure of it, but the Bible teaches that God is at work in the midst of that change and we have a role in that transformation. "God was in Christ reconciling the world to himself . . . and entrusting to us the ministry of recon-ciliation" (2 Corinthians 5:19).

Reflection Questions:
- What are some of the seasons of life you have traversed?
- What season are you in now? What season is coming?

Not in Bible #2: This too shall pass. (Sufi/Persian wisdom from the Middle Ages)

Family Activity:
Draw a tree with a trunk and bare branches. Cut out dozens of leaves. Write on the leaves what troubles or joys you are currently going through. Pin or tape the leaves on the tree. When this "season" has passed, remove the leaf and place it on the ground below the tree. Place a new leaf to give a new season you are in.

Teenage Activity:
Read a few Psalms. Maybe Psalm 8 or 88 or 23. What is your season right now? Is it happiness or is it sorrow? Write your own Psalm for the season you are in.

Adult Activity:
Where have you recently seen God in the midst of change in your life or other's lives? Share this with a neighbor or co-worker.

Prayer:
Lord, thank you for the changing of seasons, as difficult as they may be. I trust your ongoing and unchanging presence. Help me to . . .

Day 45

Not in the Bible #3: Cleanliness is next to godliness

I guess most of us are a long way from God unless we are neat-freaks or have obsessive-compulsive disorder. I don't think my mother ever said this to me, but she certainly lived it. The joke in our family was "dust never had a chance" in our house. She would blush and say it was an inheritance from the Swedish quarter of the lineage. Mom always seemed to be carrying a rag in one hand to intercept dirt before it could make a permanent home. While not in the Bible it is inspired by "Mosaic Law" and the Old Testament holiness codes where cleanliness is a great virtue. For years I thought this cleanliness was a useless rant aimed at messy teenager's rooms. Not sure how much success it had in either cleaning up the piles or in leaving our kids with a positive view of God. As I have grown older I have taken a more balanced view of this adage. Much like the Levitical codes helped our ancient ancestors in the faith practice hygiene and public health in a time ravaged by disease, personal and corporate sanitation in the 20th century have added years to the lifespan and virtually eliminated a number of ancient plagues. I draw the line, however, when we then project onto God the image of a celestial sanitation worker wagging his finger at us and scolding us if we don't pick up after ourselves. The actual phrase was coined by John Wesley, the founder of Methodism, who among other things was known for orderliness in word and deed. His brother, Charles, penned many grace-filled hymns like "Christ the Lord is Risen Today" and "Love Divine All Loves Excelling." My sister had a beautifully motto hanging in her house. It said, "Keeping a Clean House is like Shoveling during a Snow Storm." I prefer the old backpacking adage, "Pack out your trash and leave the campsite in as good (or better) shape as you found it." Not a bad motto for not only teenage rooms and households, but planet earth!

Reflection Questions:

- What areas of your life are you abundantly "OCD" (obsessive compulsive disorder) about cleanliness?
- Where have you let the dust and clutter take over your life?

Not in the Bible #3: Cleanliness is next to godliness

_____
_____
_____
_____
_____
_____
_____
_____
_____
_____
_____
_____
_____

Family Activity:

Take an afternoon or weekend together and do some cleaning up either in your home, outside or in the neighborhood.

Teenage Activity:

Where do you observe the need for cleanliness in your life and in the world? Commit to taking time and do some cleaning!

Adult Activity:

Where do you get caught up in cleanliness in your life? Where do you neglect it? Take an afternoon and address those areas in your life and in the world where you can be the change.

Prayer:

Lord, in you I am found clean and whole. Help me to not neglect my responsibilities in . . .

Day 46

Not in the Bible #4: God helps those who help themselves.

When I told my friend George Johnson that I was writing this book on Biblical "proverbial wisdom" he immediately and passionately said, "Make sure you tell people that 'God helps those who help themselves' isn't in the Bible!" I think he was saying two things: First and obviously, this phrase which many think is from the Bible actually comes from Ben Franklin's *Poor Richard's Almanac*. And many phrases we think are biblical and treat as "gospel truth" come from other sources. But, George was also saying that the sentiment or meaning behind "God helps those who help themselves" simply isn't consistent with Biblical teaching. The God of the Bible regularly helps those who don't help themselves, who mess up, who do terrible things, and who even reject him. This God is slow to anger and abounding is steadfast love. This is a God of second and third and fourth chances. I think there is another more sinister danger in how this phrase has sometimes been used in targeting poor people. The implied message is "if they just worked harder, God would help them." The God of the Bible cares for all, but has a special place in his heart for the poor. There are over 300 passages in the Bible which speak of God's care for justice for the poor."I know that the Lord will maintain the cause of the afflicted and justice for the needy" (Psalm 140:12)."Blessed are you who are poor, for yours is the kingdom of God" (Luke 6:20-21). We are also commanded to care for the poor, "If there is a poor man among you . . . you shall not harden your heart nor close your hand to your poor brother, but you shall freely open your hand and generously lend him sufficient for his needs" (Deuteronomy 15:7). Martin Luther saw that our works don't save us, but we are saved by grace through faith. In the kingdom of God no one pulls himself up by his bootstraps. We are all beggars in need of a God who helps those who can't help themselves. What amazing grace!

Reflection Questions:

- Where have you helped the poor?
- Where do you consider yourself lacking or poor?

Not in the Bible #4: God helps those who help themselves.

Family Activity:

Make small kits for the homeless. Pack a juice box, a granola bar, and a pop-open can of soup and a spoon in a plastic bag along with a favorite Bible scripture or word of encouragement and love. Next time you encounter someone asking for help, have these kits on hand to give out.

Teenage Activity:

Participate in a mission project through your church. Volunteer to help the homeless, at a soup kitchen, help an elderly neighbor.

For excellent resources on service learning check on the SALLT Project: www.sallt.org

Adult Activity:

Where can you give to the world in need? Participate in a service activity through your workplace, church, or civic organization.

Prayer:

Lord, thank you for your grace and forgiveness in my life. Help me to give and not hoard your treasure of love to . . .

Day 47

Not in the Bible #5: A fool and his money . . . are soon parted.

The Bible talks a lot about money (250 references) and fools/foolishness (200), but this isn't one of them. Even so, who could argue with the truth of this wisdom attributed to Thomas Tusson in his 1573 book *Five Hundred Pointes of Good Husbandrie?* The problem is the "fool" is always the "other guy." I am not a "fool" . . . sure I make mistakes, but "God I thank you that I am not like other people: thieves, rogues, and adulterers, even like this tax collector." Remember Jesus' words after hearing the tax collector's simple prayer, "God, be merciful to me a sinner" (Luke 18:13). Jesus said, "I tell you, this man went down to his home justified rather than the other; for all who exalt themselves will be humbled and all who humble themselves will be exalted" (Luke 18:14). We would be wise to begin our reflections on our use of money with our confession of foolishness. Communities, corporations, and nations are guilty, too. Our recent economic recession was fueled in large part by speculation in real estate and stock markets. Individuals as well as corporations made faulty (should I say foolish?) decisions based on greed and quick profits. Painfully, thousands of peoples and scores of companies have suffered because of this foolishness. So we begin our recovery with confession. Perhaps when we do we will hear with new ears, Jesus' wisdom, "Do not store up for yourselves treasures on earth, where moth and rust consume and where thieves break in and steal; but store up for yourselves treasures in heaven, where neither moth nor rust consumes and where thieves do not break in and steal. For where your treasure is, there your heart will be also" (Matthew 6:19-20).

Reflection Questions:

- What was your most recent purchase made out of want? Out of need?
- What was the last thing you gave away? Why?

Not in the Bible #5: A fool and his money . . . are soon parted.

Family Activity:

Make a list of the basic needs to survive. What are things you really don't need or use that you can give away? Find a way to do it!

Teenage Activity:

What are you tempted the most to purchase? Why? Where can you find things to recycle and to purchase recycled items? It could be clothes, books, or . . . ? Try practicing this form of recycling and giving away, rather than throwing away.

Adult Activity:

What purchases can you forgo each day? Coffee? Another dress scarf or pair of shoes? What about food? Cut back on at least one item a week and take the $ saved and donate to a worthy organization.

Prayer:

Lord, thank you for supplying my every need, and reminding me of the difference with my wants. Help me to . . .

Day 48

Not in the Bible #6: Charity begins at home.

I can still remember hearing this phrase when talking about foreign aid in college. We were discussing how the United States was way down the list of developed nations in the percentage of its Gross National Profit it contributes to help other countries. I had always thought of America as a very generous country, and yet this statistic suggested many other countries gave comparatively more than we did. One of my fellow students then raised a very interesting question. He said something like, "I think there is too much emphasis on spending our money overseas, we should take care of 'our own' first." He then said "You know the Bible says, 'Charity begins at home!'" That seemed to stop the discussion, as if God had spoken the final word. The professor asked "Where in the Bible does it say that?" The student wasn't sure, but after consulting a concordance, he had to admit his wisdom wasn't in the Bible. It actually came from Terence, a Roman comic poet, and later picked up by British writer, Sir Thomas Browne. Over the years it has become a part of common dogma. But, what is charity? Sadly, it has come to have a negative reputation as in a "charity case" being a person who becomes dependent on another person's sharing of money. In 1 Corinthians 13:13 Paul writes, "Now three things remain; faith, hope and charity, but the greatest of these is charity" (King James Version). Charity is "love." It is the heart of the Christian faith. So love begins at home. The home is the best possible incubator of love. It is where God's love in Christ is spoken and lived on a daily basis. I like to think of the household as the place we practice charity/love. It's a dress-rehearsal for the drama of living that love in the world. Charles Dickens understood this well when he said, "Charity begins at home and justice begins next door." Maybe that's how international aid begins and spreads to the whole world.

Reflection Questions:

- How do you define "charity?"
- Where have you practiced or witnessed charity lately?

_____

_____

_____

_____

_____

_____

_____

_____

_____

_____

_____

Family Activity:

Everyone take a piece of paper and cut it into a large heart shape. Now either write or draw how you practice love with your family members. Take turns sharing your paper with everyone and place on the door to you room for all to see.

Teenage Activity:

Think of a family member or close friend who needs some special care and take them out for coffee/tea/soft drink. Practice good listening skills and be a friend.

Adult Activity:

List all three elements of 1 Corinthians 13:13—faith, hope and love. Write how each has affected your life and how you have practiced and witnessed them in the world. What difference does love make?

Prayer:

Lord, thank you for your kingdom of love. Help me to . . .

Day 49

Not in the Bible #7: "I am sorry."

When was the last time you said these three simple words? They are hard to say, aren't they? If we use them, we often say "I am sorry, BUT . . ." I confess to that. Why is it so difficult? I think it goes back to the Garden of Eden when Adam and Eve ate of the tree of knowledge of good and evil. They wanted to be "god." We all do this by putting "me" first. Sin is putting ourselves at the center of our universe rather than God. Back to Eden: When God visits the garden, Adam and Eve are hiding "because they knew that they were naked" (Genesis 3:7). Like Adam and Eve, we know deep down we are wrong. Being "naked" is being vulnerable and that's scary, so we hide from God and each other. The "but" in our confession is part of our hiding and is also our way of pointing the finger and sharing the blame with someone else. But "I am sorry" is different than "we are sorry." Taking responsibility for my actions and words is an important step in becoming an adult. A counselor friend says it this way, "Control what you can control. Yourself." We begin our worship with confession for a good reason. Each of us individually "sin and fall short of the glory of God" (Romans 3:23). In saying "I am sorry" we take responsibility and open ourselves to God's forgiveness and mercy. Saying "I am sorry" is looking in the mirror after a day of work and admitting we need a bath. Confession prepares our hearts to receive God's good news of a savior in Jesus Christ. Each week in worship we practice "I am sorry" by saying "If we confess our sins, he who is faithful and just will forgive us our sins and cleanse us from all unrighteousness" (I John 9). Trusting in that merciful God, we find ourselves saying more frequently, "I am sorry!"

Reflection Questions:
- When was the last time you said "I'm sorry?"
- Was it hard or easy? Why?

Not in the
Bible #7:
"I am sorry."

_____

_____

_____

_____

_____

_____

_____

_____

_____

_____

_____

_____

_____

Family Activity:

Around the table at mealtime, make it a routine that you not only share your "highs and lows" of the day, but add an "I'm sorry" statement, too. Weave these offerings into your prayers.

Teenage Activity:

Is it hard to say "sorry"? Who do you need to apologize to in your life? For what? Go and do.

Adult Activity:

Try the simple and ancient practice of the Examen to end your day. Look back over the events of the day and offer thanks to God for those places where you were "open" to God. Then notice where you were "closed" to God and offer an "I am sorry…"

Prayer:

Lord, I confess that I am self-centered and lack focus on you and your ways of love, truth and justice. I lack the strength to admit my own faults to others and make amends. Help me to . . .

Day 50

Not in the Bible #8: "Please and thank you."

As I walked into my favorite bookstore this morning, I opened the door for an elderly gentleman. He said "thank you" and gave a brief smile. It seemed like a little thing, but little things are important. The devil may be in the details, but I believe God is often in the simple, small acts we often take for granted. This little thing is an even larger issue today because we live in a world that could be accurately described as filled with conflict. We are more polarized than ever with black vs. white, young vs. old, Republican vs. Democrat, gay vs. straight, and rich vs. poor being the norm for our adversarial society. In a civil society, however, there needs to be basic ground rules. "Please" and "thank you" are two of those simple courtesies which are fundamental to getting along with others. We humans don't use these words naturally. That's why parents begin drilling these phrases into children from an early age by asking "what do you say?" Civility takes practice But these expressions do more than that. Please is our admission that we can't do it all by ourselves . . . we need help. And thank you is our affirmation of another person's assisting us. Where are they in the Bible? All over the place. The Psalms are filled with thanksgiving and praise! Here's my favorite: "Do not worry about anything, but in everything by prayer and supplication with thanksgiving (please and thank you), let your requests be made known to God." And here's the best part: When these words become a part of how we live, "the peace of God, which surpasses all understanding, will guard your hearts and minds in Christ Jesus" (Philippians 4: 6-7).

Reflection Questions:

- What forms of etiquette were drilled into you during your childhood?
- Can you remember the last time you used "please" or "thank you?" When was it? For what reason?

Family Activity:
How do you say "thank you" to others? Some use words, some use gifts or service, even touch. What type do you like to use? What way do you like to receive? Share with your family members.

Teenage Activity:
Who do you need to thank? From whom do you need to ask for assistance? Write 3 personalized thank you cards (or email) to people who have helped you. Cultivate an attitude of gratitude!

Adult Activity:
What do you commonly worry about? What do you take to God in prayer? Is it only "needs" or "wants?" Try starting every prayer with thanksgiving.

Prayer:
Dear Lord, thank you for your grace and mercy. Thank you for your patience and guiding Spirit in my life. Lord, I realize that I have needs too. Please, Lord, help me . . .

A Final Byte

Practice makes perfect!

MRS. CHAVEZ, MY PIANO TEACHER

Practice does not make perfect. Only perfect practice makes perfect.

VINCE LOMBARDI

Finally, brothers and sisters, whatever is true, whatever is noble, whatever is right, whatever is pure, whatever is lovely, whatever is admirable—if anything is excellent or praiseworthy—think about such things. 9 Whatever you have learned or received or heard from me, or seen in me—put it into practice. And the God of peace will be with you.

PHILIPPIANS 4:8-9 (N.I.V)

Made in the USA
Charleston, SC
18 November 2014